FOOTLOOSE AROUND PUGET SOUND

100 Walks on Beaches, Lowlands, and Foothills

Text: Janice Krenmayr

Photos: Bob and Ira Spring

Maps: Helen Sherman

THE MOUNTAINEERS · SEATTLE

THE MOUNTAINEERS

Organized 1906

To explore and study the mountains, forests and watercourses of the Northwest;

To gather into permanent form the history and traditions of this region;

To preserve by the encouragement of protective legislation or otherwise the natural beauty of Northwest America;

To make expeditions into these regions in fulfillment of the above purposes;

To encourage a spirit of good fellowship among all lovers of outdoor life.

Fourth Edition, revised March 1974

Copyright © 1969
The Mountaineers, Seattle, Washington 98111
P. O. Box 122

Manufactured in the United States of America by
Craftsman Press, Inc.
Seattle, Washington

Book design by Marge Mueller

Library of Congress Catalog Card No. 76-103697

Cover photo: Fall leaves in Seward Park—Hike 8

Title photo: Mount Baker and Big Lake from Devil's Mountain Lookout—Hike 24

Page 18: Forest in Seward Park—Hike 8

Photos of Lake Elizabeth (Hike 37), Sunday Lake (Hike 49)
and Carbon Ridge Lookout (Hike 75). By Janice Krenmayr.

WALKERS OF THE WORLD, UNITE!

In 1964, when this book was conceived by the Literary Fund Committee of The Mountaineers, the gasoline machine seemed to be completing an uncontested conquest of a craven America and none of us held any immediate hope for a counterattack. We nevertheless moved ahead, believing that before the masses could be aroused into barricading the streets they must be inflamed by radical manifestos.

By publication in 1969 we already knew we were not alone, what with agitators here and there rallying guerrilla bands to harass highwaymen, and a scattering of elected officials beginning to wonder if automobiles really voted. Since 1969 a series of limited yet significant victories have encouraged us to hope the arrogance of machines may indeed be successfully challenged short of Armageddon. This edition is therefore not a forlorn howl amid freeway roar but a confident call for new recruits to the winning side, the people side.

Contrary to what many of us thought while dismally observing the proliferation of automobiles and motorcycles and snowmobiles and dune buggies and swamp buggies and all-terrain vehicles, the nation's legs have not atrophied. In 1965 the federal Bureau of Outdoor Recreation estimated the annual total of pleasure walks taken by Americans had risen since 1960 from 566 million to 1.3 billion.

In Washington, the state Interagency Committee for Outdoor Recreation estimates that in 1970 there were 32 million "people-occasions" of walking for pleasure, exceeded among outdoor recreation activities only by bicycling (60 million), driving (44 million), and swimming (42 million) and far overshadowing fishing (13 million), watching outdoor sports (12 million), boating (11 million), skiing and other snow sports (4 million), and hunting (2.6 million).

Following pages thus hardly represent the revival of a lost art. Americans never have given up walking—for convenience, for health, for pleasure, for sanity. However, many are so isolated by a confusion of highways and streets they don't know where to go for a happy hike. Our intent is to lead the way.

What This Book Is, and Isn't

Other Mountaineer guidebooks (see the back cover) describe hikes in mountains rising above Puget Sound. Lowlands are the theme here—mainly, close-to-home walks prefaced by short drives or none, on paths open all or most of the year. Though delightful any time, these trips are particularly good for summer evenings and winter Sundays.

The selection is specifically for people of Puget Sound City, the Everett-to-Olympia sprawl. A resident of Sedro Woolley, Port Angeles, Ellensburg, or Chehalis can leave his front door and in minutes be sniffing wildflowers and hearing birdsongs; he needs no help in finding pleasant strolls. A megalopolitan, however, may be so disoriented he imagines escape is impossible without getting in the car and driving driving driving to a national forest or national park.

Most of the walks herein are on beaches or in urban and suburban parks; some climb foothills of the Olympics and Cascades; a few probe mountain valleys. None requires the slightest training nor any special equipment, though many are more pleasant with boots, canteen, extra clothing for wind and rain, and a rucksack to carry lunch and camera.

The 100 trips are just a sampling; a great many more await exploration by the curious walker once his imagination has been stimulated. Janice Krenmayr, author-publisher of the two volumes of **Footloose in Seattle,** made the selection after studying the generations of experience summarized in files of the Trail Trips Committee of The Mountaineers, talking to hikers in and out of the club, and finally walking all the 100—and dozens more she for one reason or another rejected.

Ideally none of the trips would be polluted by the racket of exploding gasoline vapors, but in these early years of the pedestrian revolt foot-only paths simply are too few. Some routes must be shared, for a while, with cars and motorcycles, and that's a shame. However, be of good cheer, for restrictions on the virtually unlimited license of machines to go where they please, plus the dedication of new walking corridors, will steadily enlarge the realm of peace and quiet. Some future edition of this book will be uncompromisingly gasoline-free.

Motorcycles are certain to be expelled ultimately from natural areas because the majority of the trail-riders are so oblivious to common courtesy and other people's rights that wherever they razz they engender hostility.

Unfortunately, legpower does not automatically imply saintliness; if the sport is to thrive, each hiker must learn good outdoor manners. Such as: Do not litter—carry home all garbage. Do not eliminate body wastes at random, particularly in populated areas—take care of needs before and after the walk, and if caught short, be as courteous as a cat. Do not dig clams and pick flowers and collect pretty rocks—take home nothing but photographs and memories and garbage. Do not yell and scream and holler as if nobody else shared the planet—be unobtrusive. In summary, be **clean and quiet and respectful.** And finally, if when following a route described herein you encounter a new sign saying "Private Property—No Trespassing," turn back, choose another trail—and curse the bad manners of your predecessors.

A warning: On trips outside cities and parks, beware of hunting season. Inexperienced gunners who prowl close-to-city areas are such a menace they effectively forbid these lands to walkers (and sane hunters).

The Continuing Offensive by the Machines

Despite glad tidings of recent years the walkers' millenium is not at hand, nor will it come without the efforts of a multitude.

The Great American Freeway Revolt has reached Puget Sound and the highway gang has been thwarted in several plots. But its sacrosanct funding remains intact and though schools deteriorate and people go hungry the bulldozers and earthmovers and pavers are as busy as ever. If guerrillas halt one road the money is diverted to another project and concretization continues at an unreduced pace.

Ingenious manufacturers are ever-busy spawning an unholy breed of noisy toys. From minibikes employed by infants to give a horrid new meaning to the "children's hour," to machismo-boosters of the motorcycle-man, there is a quiet-wrecker for every ecological niche the automobile cannot occupy.

Suburbs and vacation-home subdivisions creep over the countryside like scabies, closing beaches and crushing forests and creeks and marshes. It is a brave politician who timidly suggests the destruction should be slowed; none except those wishing a quick return to private life dares demand an instant and total halt to development, a thoughtful moratorium, and a carefully-reasoned resumption based on zero population growth and extremely selective economic growth.

What does it all mean to walkers? Further chapters in the old story—the infantry obliterated by the panzers.

Join the Counterattack!

Machines admittedly must be granted a place, but a quick scan of a Puget Sound road map proves we needn't worry about opportunities for pleasure-driving. The automobile remains indispensable to recreational walking in outlying areas, although public transit systems are expanding to connect downtown and trailheads. Notable in this regard is the operation of Metro Transit, begun on January 1, 1973, by the Municipality of Metropolitan Seattle, designed as a county-wide bus system to serve all cities and towns in King County as well as the unincorporated urban and rural areas, and to connect with Tacoma, Everett, and the ferry system across Puget Sound. To request a map of the new Metro Transit system, call 583-4844.

The critical problem of the moment is to sharply curtail off-road machines. First, they are intolerant of the rights of others, both the noise and the speed disturbing the peace of hikers and horsemen and menacing their health. Second, Earth has become a very small planet; we cannot create more land but we can prevent the shrinkage of what we have. Just as motorboats make lakes smaller and sailboats and canoes make them larger, machines shorten trails and walking lengthens them. Third, energy consumption must decrease; recreation vehicles are not the wave of the future but the last gasp of the feckless past.

Motorcycles will continue to have unrestricted use of automobile roads and of the thousands of miles of low-standard logging tracks in the Olympics and Cascades. It may be appropriate to set aside lowland "motorcycle parks"— if locations can be found where the neighbors do not object. But this is **all** the motorcycles can be allowed and they must be **totally banned** from **every** trail, including those of national forests.

Sharing top priority with pest control is establishment of a lowland trail system. Mountain trails, of which we have a plenty except in the foothills and front ranges, are open only part of the year, demand a disproportionate amount of driving for an afternoon or evening stroll, and are not easily available to people of limited mobility, those who are too young or too poor to own automobiles. In any event, near-home walking is the sport of choice. The most-used recreational terrain in Washington, by a wide margin, is urban trails, which in 1970 served 43 million people-occasions of hiking, horse-riding, and bicycling, mostly in Central Puget Sound (the area covered by this book) where 57 percent of the state's population lives.

Despite the steady destruction of trails by subdivisions and logging roads, many still exist— but on borrowed time. Some Janice surveyed for the first edition could not be included because they crossed private land, the owners saying they didn't mind a few hikers but would react to Sunday crowds by erecting "No Trespassing" signs. Several walks described in the first edition have been dropped from this one. In a few years the only paths open to the public will be those in public trail systems.

Trail corridors can be established by several methods. One is land purchase—preferably before subdividers draw near and speculators drive the price skyhigh. A second is to buy or condemn easements, as along rivers and lakeshores; bluffs, ravines, and marshes unattractive to builders provide excellent trail routes even through densely-inhabited areas. A third is to "perfect" public right of passage over private land on routes used for generations; owners have been illegally blocking historic paths and in the absence of challenge have been getting away with it. Finally, abandoned railways and the rights-of-way of powerlines and telephone cables and pipelines offer innumerable walking and horse-riding and bicycling lanes.

As will be discussed in the next section, federal, state, and local governments are developing plans to do these very things.

However, wonderful as it is to have a new breed of imaginative and idealistic public servants dedicated to enlarging the pedestrian world, without citizen backing their plans will never leave paper: not every trail will be unopposed; subdividers are scanning the planned paths with steely eyes and the machine lobby is gunning its motor, preparing for a battle to the death.

Citizen groups initiated the pedestrian revolt. The prophets who led toward protection of the Green River Gorge and creation of the Sammamish River Park (and future trail) and the Burke-Gilman Trail endured discouraging years when nobody listened, nobody cared. The way to repay our debt to the pioneers is to follow their example.

This is an exciting period in Puget Sound history, a time when anyone can share—and a great many **must** share—in shaping the pedestrian future. To do so, a walker (or bicyclist, or horseman) can join an organization committed to supporting the trail concept in general, and/or one focused on a particular new trail. More than that, any individual can personally become a trail-creator.

If **you** know a neglected opportunity, walk the route, take photos, catalog the attractions, investigate ownership. Prepare a plan, draw a map. Assemble a committee of neighbors and friends, choose a name, have letterhead printed —and start writing letters. Tell the story to conservation and outdoor organizations and ask their endorsements and assistance. Present your scheme to the proper public officials. Organize "hike-ins" to dramatize the issue and gain newspaper and television publicity. By such means you, too, can contribute to a footloose future around Puget Sound.

March 1973   Harvey Manning

THE FOOTLOOSE FUTURE AROUND THE SOUND

This edition of **Footloose** comes in a time of rapid change. The next edition doubtless will be considerably different as old trails are lost to suburbs, logging, and "No Trespassing" signs and as the new public trail systems are expanded.

Following pages offer a glimpse of the future from the vantage of March 1973, first discussing government agencies involved in trail planning and construction and then briefly noting paths opened too late for inclusion in the body of the book, others expected to be completed during the next decade (if walkers work for them), certain "trespassing" hikes that ought to be legalized, and a sampling of dreams.

GOVERNMENT AGENCIES AT WORK

The federal Bureau of Outdoor Recreation administers the Land and Water Conservation Fund which since 1965 has supplied matching grants to state and local governments. The 1968 National Trails System Act envisions paths extending the full width and breadth of the nation but especially stresses those in and near urban centers.

In 1964 Washington state voters approved Initiative 215 creating the Interagency Committee for Outdoor Recreation (IAC) and the Outdoor Recreation Account, funded by bond issues and other sources, including the federal Land and Water Conservation Fund. The IAC is charged to provide outdoor recreation resources in a manner to maximize preservation of the natural quality of the environment, provide public recreation facilities, assist local governments, and encourage programs to promote outdoor recreation and proper husbandry of recreation resources. The committee consists of five citizen members (appointed by the Governor) and the directors of seven state agencies: Departments of Commerce and Economic Development, Ecology, Fisheries, Game, Highways, Natural Resources, and the Parks and Recreation Commission. The IAC grants funds to state and local agencies for projects compatible with the Washington Statewide Comprehensive Outdoor Recreation and Open Space Plan (SCORP), a plan constantly revised since 1965, serving all levels of government, and giving private citizens a means of direct involvement through comments.

In accordance with the 1970 State Recreation Trails System Act, in 1973 the IAC completed a State Recreational Trails Systems Plan. Access to water is particularly emphasized, for though Washington has 2337 miles of marine shoreline, less than 10 percent is devoted to recreation; 1000 miles are in state ownership but only a small portion is usable by the public due to access closures by owners of adjacent uplands. As of 1971, the state has ceased selling public tidelands and shorelands, as was done until then by the Department of Natural Resources.

In 1972 the Legislature enacted a law devoting 0.5 percent of state motor vehicle registration fees to providing hiking and bicycling paths along highways whenever roads are reconstructed or relocated. In the same year the All-Terrain Vehicles and Snowmobile Act provided funds from permit fees and a portion of the gasoline tax to acquire, develop, maintain, and control vehicle use of nonhighway roads, ATV trails, and areas for recreational use. (A nonhighway road is defined as any road other than a highway generally capable of travel by a conventional two-wheel-drive passenger automobile during most of the year, provided such roads were not built or maintained by appropriations from the motor vehicle fund.) It is expected that most of these funds will be used for the maintenance of roads which will benefit all who drive on the backroads—including hikers—rather than for the construction of ATV trails; the machine-men, however, have other ideas.

Four state agencies build and maintain trails. State parks, of course, contain numerous paths. The Department of Natural Resources, though oriented to income-producing uses (logging, grazing, and the like) of state land it administers, is showing increasing concern for recreation, mostly of the motorized variety but including such noble works as relocation of the popular Mt. Si trail when logging on private land wiped out the old route. The Game Department for years has been purchasing land and easements on streams and lakes, in many cases providing opportunities for hiking as well as fishing and hunting. The Highway Department has begun planning walking and bicycling paths along highway corridors.

In October 1971 the King County Department of Planning completed an Urban Trails Plan which will be implemented by the Department of Community Development, Division of Parks and Recreation. The plan contains 621 miles of trails, devoted 66 percent to pedestrians, 22 percent of bicycles, 8 percent to horses, and 4 percent to "other." Since King County has a third of the state's population, mostly in the western third of the county, the urban trail system will be the largest in the state. Motorized use will not be allowed; three motorcycle parks are planned at sites yet to be selected, opening scheduled for about 1977. As of early 1973, the King County Council was considering an ordinance that would require pedestrian easements along lakes, rivers, and creeks whenever any change is made in land use.

In 1971 the Snohomish County Parks and Recreation Department completed a trail plan with 150 miles for pedestrians, equestrians, and bicyclists, compared to an existing 4 miles. Trails mainly will be located on land unlikely to be developed, such as floodplains and hillsides; as much as possible rights-of-way will be acquired in outlying areas prior to their urbanization.

The Pierce County Parks and Recreation Department expects to finish an inventory of recreation lands about 1974.

The three counties are coordinating efforts and many trails will cross boundaries without interruption.

Cities and towns also are planning trail systems cooperatively with the counties. In 1973 the Seattle Department of Community Development issued a preliminary Linear Open Space Report identifying opportunities for greenbelts and trails along ravines, streams, powerline rights-of-way, and undeveloped streets. The intent is to meet standards of the federal Bureau of Outdoor Recreation which suggest 25 miles of foot trails and 25 miles of bicycle trails for each 50,000 people.

Virtually every path noted here connects to others; when all systems are complete a person will be able to walk throughout the several

counties on routes barred to gasoline machines.

Note: Bicycle paths in the plans are not described here unless they are also designed for pedestrians.

SEATTLE VICINITY

Fort Lawton

In 1972 the city obtained 391 acres of Fort Lawton for a park. Woodland paths are planned. Bluffs will be left largely undisturbed. At low tide a several-mile beach walk can be taken from Elliott Bay around West Point to Shilshole Bay.

A future trail will connect Fort Lawton Park to Kiwanis Ravine, an undeveloped park, and the Ballard Locks, there joining the Burke-Gilman Trail.

Burke-Gilman Trail, Lake Washington Loop

In 1973 the Burlington-Northern Railroad abandoned its line from Interstate 5 bridge across Lake Union, through the University of Washington campus, north near Lake Washington to Kenmore. Seattle has obtained the 9 miles within the city for recreational use; the right-of-way north to Kenmore still must be acquired by King County. Hopefully the sections from Ballard Locks to I-5 and Kenmore to Woodinville also will become a trail if and when abandoned by the railroad.

The Lake Washington Loop, a 51-mile route around the lake, the Burke-Gilman Trail being one section, will tie many parks together, including Sand Point when the city obtains the air station, and will connect to many other trails.

Thornton Creek Trail

Several miles up a lovely, largely-natural stream from Burke-Gilman Trail to Thornton Creek Park. A branch trail ultimately will connect to Green Lake.

Puget Sound Trail

A grand plan shared by three counties and a number of cities for a trail extending 65 miles from Tacoma to Mukilteo, beside or near the water the whole way, linking dozens of parks and connecting to trails leading inland. Beach-strolling, views over the Sound to the Olympics, creeks tumbling down wild ravines. The key to the scheme is the eventual abandonment by Burlington-Northern of its sealevel line in favor of one farther east. Most of the route is walkable now, following tracks or, at low tide, the beach, but illegally: unwary pedestrians risk their lives and limbs and the company cannot officially condone public use without accepting liability. However, thousands of people regularly trespass from unadvertised access points. Over a period of years I have hiked most of the way from Seattle to Mukilteo and the only occasion I was challenged was a blacked-out night in 1942 when soldiers detained me on suspicion of being a Japanese spy.

Duwamish Ridge

Traversing the wooded bluff above the Duwamish valley, 6 miles in length, passing the isolated ravine of Puget Park.

Beacon Ridge

From Seattle to Renton, 11 miles along a Seattle City Light transmission line. Walkable now, though not formally open.

Shoreline Trail

From Puget Sound Trail 8 miles up Boeing Creek ravine, by Ronald Bog Park, to Burke-Gilman Trail at Lake Forest Park. Would tie to the proposed Highlands Park, a square mile of virgin forest recently abandoned as a watershed. For years I roamed the wilderness of what we called the "Boeing Tract," until it was logged during World War II, then subdivided; I only just learned a portion has been spared—perhaps I can, after all, go home again.

Shoreline Lakes Loop

Linking Haller and Bitter Lakes in Seattle, Echo Lake in Shoreline, and Lake Ballinger in Snohomish County, 11 miles in all.

NORTH OF SEATTLE

Swamp Creek Trail

Some 9 miles, in two counties, along Swamp Creek east of Mountlake Terrace and Lynnwood.

Picnic Point—Cascade Crest

A route from Picnic Point Park, on the Sound 3 miles north of Edmonds (1000 feet of beach and 2 miles of trails now open), to the mountains. Composed of: 8-mile Picnic Point Trail to J.E. McCollum Park, connecting to Swamp Creek Trail; 9-mile Clearview Trail along a pipeline easement; 3-mile Three Rivers Trail up the Tualco Valley; 21-mile High Rock Trail paralleling the Skykomish River on the south side from High Rock to a bridge east of Gold Bar, then north of the river on abandoned county roads to Index; national forest trails to the Cascade Crest and the Pacific Crest National Scenic Trail.

Kayak Point—Fall City

Beginning on saltwater at Kayak Point Park, 14 miles north of Everett, with 3000 feet of beach and several miles of future trails, joining routes to the mountains. Composed of: 5-mile Kayak Point Trail connecting state and county parks; 9-mile path through Tulalip Reservation to Marysville; 25 miles along banks of Ebey Slough and Snohomish and Snoqualmie Rivers to King County line; 22 miles more along the Snoqualmie to Fall City, there meeting other trails.

Flowing Lake—Monte Cristo

From lowlands to mountains: 26-mile Flowing Lake Loop utilizing powerline and pipeline easements and state forest lands southeast of Lake Stevens, north and east of Snohomish; 14-mile Pilchuck River Trail to O'Reilly Acres Park near Granite Falls; eastward along abandoned line of Hartford and Eastern Railroad (last trains ran in the early 1930s) up the South Fork Stillaguamish River; national forest trails to the 1890s mining town of Monte Cristo and to the Glacier Peak Wilderness.

Flowing Lake—Darrington

Also from lowlands to mountains: Flowing Lake Loop; 14-mile Wietas Trail north on pipeline easement to Arlington; up the North Fork Stillaguamish River (2½ miles of trail now open, beginning 2 miles east of Arlington) to Darrington; national forest trails to the Cascade Crest.

Pacific Ocean—Rocky Mountains

A national scenic trail has been proposed that would begin on Olympic National Park ocean beaches, cross the peninsula, connect by ferry to Whidbey Island, proceed up Fidalgo Island to the Mt. Vernon vicinity, and lead via the Skagit or Nooksack River into the North Cascades, then through the Okanogan Highlands to the Selkirks and the Rocky Mountain National Scenic Trail.

EAST OF SEATTLE

Bothell—Duvall: Tolt Pipeline Trail

The first King County trail, opened January 1973, following Seattle City Water pipeline. Begins at Blythe Park on the Sammamish River at Bothell, climbs over Norway Hill, Hollywood Hill, and Bear Creek Plateau, drops to the Snoqualmie River at Duvall, total 11 miles.

Connecting and related trails planned: Norway Hill to Juanita Beach Park, 5 miles; Kirkland—Bear Creek—Redmond—Marymoor Park, 15 miles; Ames Lake—Tolt Hill, linking Patterson Creek and Tolt Park, 3 miles.

Sammamish River Trail and Lake Sammamish Loop

Along the stream 13 miles from Blythe Park in Bothell through Sammamish River Park to Marymoor Park. A 20-mile around-the-lake loop including the state park, connecting to Lake Washington Loop and other trails.

Stossel Creek—Tolt River

South through the woodland valley of Stossel Creek to its mouth on the Tolt River, then down the Tolt to the Snoqualmie River at Carnation, 14 miles. Passes the 6900-acre Marckworth Forest, administered by the University of Washington. The old trail up the Tolt to the forks could be reopened for a side-trip.

Seattle—Cascade Crest

A major element of the state trail system, 61 miles from Seattle to the Cascade Crest. From Lakeside Avenue in Seattle over the Mercer Island Floating Bridge, north through Mercer Slough and Bellefields Park to Houghton, through Bridle Trails State Park to Marymoor Park, 15 miles; across the ridge to the Snoqualmie River, perhaps partly following the historic Lake Washington—Tolt River road, begun in 1873, mostly abandoned but still in public ownership, then upstream to Snoqualmie Falls, 20 miles; along river dikes to the Middle Fork Snoqualmie River and on national forest trails to Dutch Miller Gap in the proposed Alpine Lakes Wilderness.

Renton—Woodinville

Along a transmission line about 1½ miles east of and paralleling Highway 405, total 23 miles. The line and trail continue north into Snohomish County. Not legally walkable now.

Wilburton—Phantom Lake

Through some of Bellevue's last remaining open space, 4 miles.

May Creek—Cougar Mountain, Lake Washington—Cougar Mountain

As of this writing I can step out my door and roam for hours in wild woodlands of Cougar Mountain, the largest natural area so close to Seattle. A dozen years ago many square miles could have been purchased for the cost of 30 seconds worth of freeway, but public agencies weren't thinking ahead and now the approach of the urban frontier has driven the price out of sight. Surveyors' stakes declare my backyard wilderness is doomed. However, if plans become reality portions of the mountain will be saved for walking.

The 11-mile path from May Creek to Cougar Mountain will begin at Renton, proceed to May

Creek Park, by Lake Boren, through Newcastle, a coal-mining town once larger than Seattle, to Coal Creek Park. The 5-mile Coal Creek Trail will go from Newcastle Park on Lake Washington, up the greenery-tangled ravine of Coal Creek, to the county park on the summit of Cougar Mountain. A continuation will descend to Lake Sammamish Park. The 3-mile Lake Kathleen Trail will connect May Creek to the Cedar River.

Renton—Fall City

From Renton up May Creek to Issaquah, passing between Cougar and Squak Mountains and side-trails to their tops, up Patterson Creek between Beaver Lake and Grand Ridge, down to Fall City on the Snoqualmie River; total 15 miles.

Issaquah Creek

From Lake Sammamish Park south along Issaquah Creek, past side-trails up Tiger and Squak Mountains, to Hobart, 12 miles.

Tiger Mountain—Squak Mountain State Park

If Cougar Mountain has been lost through neglect, its neighbors in the "Issaquah Alps" have not—not yet—and offer a fantastic opportunity for an enormous state park with a rich and varied empire of equestrian and pedestrian paths accessible by Metro Transit from every urban center in King County. The idea has gained momentum from the Bullitt family's gift to the State Parks Commission of 590 acres on the north side of Squak, a provision of the gift being that the area must be kept natural—no buildings, no motorized vehicles. Other public land on Squak, including the county-owned summit, could be added to the Bullitt property. Adjacent private land must be acquired—and before it is logged off—to realize the full potential.

Tiger Mountain—the summit 3000 feet high, the same elevation as Snoqualmie Pass, and standing abruptly above Issaquah—is partly state land, partly private. The road to the top is described in this book but a number of existing trails cannot be mentioned because they are to some extent "trespassing" routes. The moun-tain is spacious enough for a 100-mile trail system.

Where is the citizen group that will pursue the dream of the Squak-Tiger State Park? Where is the public official wishing to share with the Bullitts the gratitude of posterity?

Covington—Fall City

From Big Soos Creek (see below) to Maple Valley to Hobart, side-trails up Tiger and Taylor Mountains, via Deep Creek ravine to the Raging River, and downstream to Fall City on the Snoqualmie River, there meeting trails north along the river and east to the mountains. Total, 25 miles.

North Bend Area

Wolf Bauer, who led the campaign to preserve Green River Gorge, has said, "In any other state the North Bend area would be a national park—we just don't appreciate what we have." A few of the nearby hikes are described in this book but many more could be developed. The footstool peaks of Rattlesnake Ledge, Herpicide Spire, Little Si, and Fuller Mountain provide marvelous views of mountains and valleys. These short summit ascents, longer ones of Si, Teneriffe, and Defiance, and a network of forest and river paths would make North Bend a major all-year recreation area easily reached by Metro Transit.

The Checkerboard and the Tree Farms

Between lowland trail systems and Forest Service trails in the high Cascades lies the muddled mess of the "checkerboard," where public and private ownership alternate in mile-square blocks. The maddening mixture is the result of the nefarious Northern Pacific Land Grant, called by a Congressional committee of the 1920s the worst theft in the history of the nation, making the Teapot Dome scandal look like pinching nickels from petty cash. Rational management is impossible and both timber companies and the Forest Service log with little if any concern for preserving trails traveled continuously since Indian days. Establishment of the Alpine Lakes National Recreation Area, centered on a Wilderness Area, would help unscramble the confusion. Outraged citizens from Montana to Seattle feel the final solution of this and similar problems must be "revestment" of the land grant—that is, returning the stolen goods to the public domain.

At the edge of the lowlands and extending into the mountain checkerboard are private "tree farms" with a tremendous recreation potential. However, free enterprise cannot supply free recreation, and fees to support campgrounds and trails are impractical because of the surrounding no-charge public lands. Whether by acquisition of the tree farms in their entirety, or by obtaining easements over which national, state, and county trails can be built, this massive resource cannot continue to be neglected. Meanwhile, there is fairly quiet walking on tree-farm logging roads, mostly closed to cars because of the truck hazard. Signs on Weyerhaeuser road gates specifically invite pedestrians but bar motorcyclists (some of whom ignore the signs, go around the gates, and have earned for themselves—and their brethren—an evil reputation as vandals and pyromaniacs and thieves).

WEST OF SEATTLE

Puget Sound beach-walking is in a crisis period. Most of us have assumed the tide-swept sands belonged to everyone. How can an individual "own" a beach? That's like claiming the moon and stars. But many popular beaches **are** "private" and the "owners" increasingly resent intrusions. We surely sympathize, but what about those of us who cannot afford a piece of beach— and anyway share the Indian ethic that all land and all water belong to all people, all animals, all plants, in common? Are we to be denied what we have always considered our heritage as Puget Sounders? Are we, like the Indians, to be crowded together on tiny "reservations?"

The legal situation is unclear. Experts judge the zone below mean high tide to have been continuously traveled so long (thousands of years!) that the public right of passage is inalienable. However, courts have not settled the issue

and some "owners" are closing "their" beaches —or trying to.

Vashon Island Loop

The King County trail plan does include one superb beach walk, 32 miles around Vashon Island, on or near waterfront the whole way. Reached by ferry from Seattle or Tacoma.

SOUTH OF SEATTLE

Puget Sound Trail—Inland

The following trails are planned leading inland from the shores of Puget Sound: Miller Creek to Riverton and Duwamish River Trail, 6 miles; Shorewood to Duwamish River, 6 miles; Des Moines to Green River, 5 miles from Des Moines Park up the delightful ravine, by Angle Lake; Saltwater Park to Kent on the Green River, 3 miles; Redondo to Auburn on the Green River, 8 miles.

Duwamish—Green—Cedar Rivers Loop, Interurban Trail

At 69 miles, the longest trail planned for the King County system, from south Seattle to the Green River Gorge, then north along the Cedar River to the Lake Washington Loop for a return to Seattle. Parts are open now and described in this book.

In 1972 Puget Sound Power and Light Co. opened to hikers, horsemen, and bicyclists a 6½-mile stretch from Kent south, following the long-abandoned right-of-way of the Seattle-Tacoma Interurban Railway. Eventually the trail will go 26 miles to Milton in Pierce County.

Green Valley Bluff

Along the steep, wooded valley wall dropping from Federal Way plateau to the Green River, 14 miles.

Big Soos Creek

The future county park at Big Soos will be a major trail hub: Covington—Fall City (see above); 18 miles from Cedar River to Green River, through wild and lovely Big Soos gorge; Benson Hill Trail, connecting the Kent—Renton Trail to Big Soos Creek, 4 miles; from Canyon Park in Kent past Lake Meridian Park to Big Soos Creek, 5 miles.

White River

Pacific to Enumclaw to Mud Mountain Dam, 24 miles, tying into the Naches Pass wagon road up the Greenwater River, the route by which emigrants of the 1850s descended from the Cascades.

Cascade Foothills

Enumclaw to the Green River Gorge, 15 miles.

Fort Lewis Prairies

Miles and miles of paths once were open to the public in the vast Fort Lewis reservation. Partly because of the Southeast Asia War but mainly because supervision became too much trouble, the post was closed to civilians—though by advance application organized groups sometimes can gain permission for trips. Meanwhile, a large portion of the prairies has been leased for cattle grazing, and there go the flowers. Eventually the military may depart, leaving us a huge regional park. Hold the happy thought.

Nisqually Delta to Mount Rainier

The Nisqually River flows from glaciers in Mount Rainier National Park to one of Puget Sound's two largest, mostly-natural deltas. Though the estuary cries out for a wildlife refuge, the Ports of Tacoma and Olympia want to build a superport there instead; they so far have been rebuffed by the environmentalist militia, but scheme on. A glorious plan has been suggested to keep the entire river virtually pristine in a series of parks and special-management zones; a byproduct could be a trail from saltwater to glaciers. Striving to achieve such dreams as this, we may truly build a New Jerusalem in Puget Sound's green and pleasant land.

March 1973   H. M.

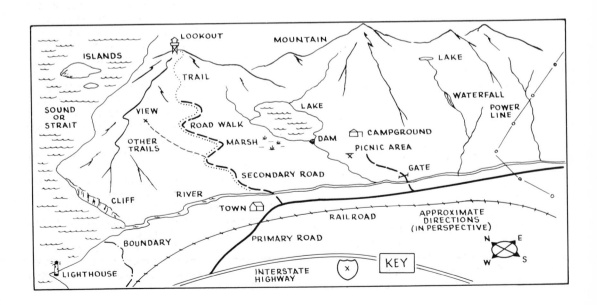

ACKNOWLEDGMENTS

No book like this one materializes through the efforts of a writer, photographer, or artist alone. Each of us is pulled along by a chain of helping hands. A most rewarding part of the seemingly endless treadmill of traveling, sorting, and recording data is memories of individual kindnesses, from the thoughtful farmer who dipped cool water from a hidden spring on a blistering day to government and company officials who kept us in mind and apprised us of changes and aspects that affected the book.

To list all the links on the chain would be impossible. Thanks are due to district rangers of Mount Rainier National Park and Mount Baker, Snoqualmie, and Olympic National Forests, the Department of Natural Resources, State Parks and Recreation Commission, State Highway Department, King County Parks, State Game Department, and to those in various timber companies who eased the path in various ways.

Special thanks are due to Joe Witt of the University of Washington Arboretum, Jay Becker and Howard Millan of Weyerhaeuser Company and Robert McAdam of St. Regis Company, Edwin Glueck and Mary Haire of Tacoma, Mrs. Clyde Davidson of Steilacoom, Mr. and Mrs. William Bartels of Alder, Mr. and Mrs. Wayne Richardson of Seattle, Bill and Virginia Cowling of Seattle, and deep appreciation, as always, to old standby friends like Don Sherwood of the Seattle Park Department, Mrs. Bernice Kreps of the Seattle Transit System, Bernice Paull, Audrey Houck, and Sandra Freeman of the Seattle TIMES Information Department who cheerfully dug in when detailed research was needed.

For help and encouragement we are grateful to Harvey Manning, Tom Miller, Marge Mueller, Grace Kent, and the Literary Fund Committee and of course to our patient and enduring spouses for their continual assistance.

Finally, to readers and hikers who follow these trails; who marvel with the same ecstatic awe at the tiniest leaf of delicate mosses to the grandest mountain and leave it all behind WITHOUT CHANGE for others to admire, our heartfelt thanks. If, through this book, one more youngster, one more adult, becomes aware of such beauty and thrills to the exquisite harmony that makes it all possible, then it is well worth the effort. For awareness is the first step; then follows understanding and cooperation in preserving such balance through wise and skillful integration of man and his doubtful mores.

Hopefully, not too late.

Janice Krenmayr
Bob and Ira Spring
Helen Sherman

THE MOUNTAINEERS: AN INVITATION

The Mountaineers, with groups based in Seattle, Everett, Tacoma, and Olympia (and groups elsewhere in the planning stage) warmly invite the membership of all lovers of outdoor life who sympathize with the purposes of the organization and wish to share its activities.

The Mountaineers sponsor a year-around program of climbing, hiking, camping, ski touring, and snowshoeing. Many hundreds of outings are scheduled each year, ranging from afternoon walks to trips lasting 2 weeks or more. On a typical weekend as many as 50 excursions may be offered, from ocean beaches to the summit of Mount Rainier. In addition, members engage in countless privately-organized trips of all kinds; the opportunity is boundless to make new friends with similar interests.

Enjoying wildlands is one side of the coin; the other is working to preserve the natural beauty of Northwest America. Here, The Mountaineers continue their role of leadership as they have for more than 60 years.

For a membership application, and further information on club activities, write The Mountaineers, P.O. Box 122, Seattle, Washington 98111.

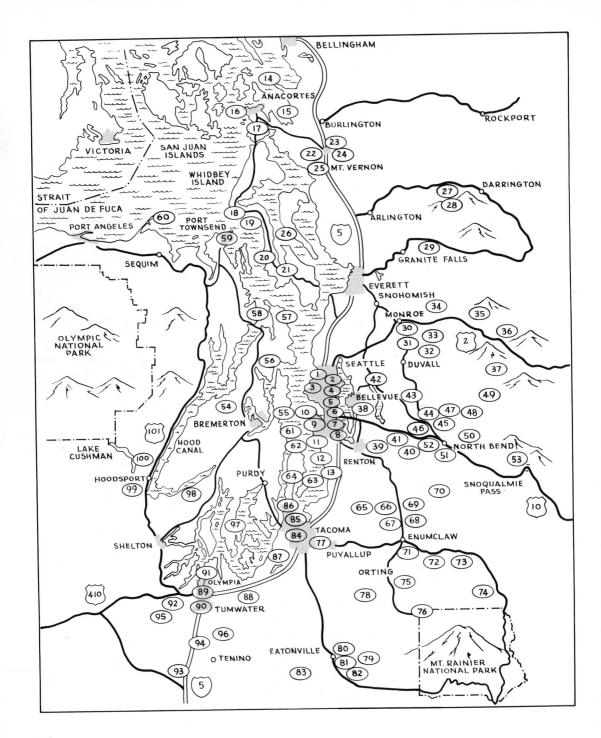

TABLE OF CONTENTS

FOOTLOOSE AROUND PUGET SOUND

100 Walks on Beaches, Lowlands, and Foothills

1 GREEN LAKE

A San Francisco housewife, accompanying her husband on a business trip, answered promptly when queried her personal plans for diversion:

"First I'm going to walk around Green Lake."

She had never been to Seattle, but she knew about Green Lake—the one "people can walk all around." It is a favorite with many Seattleites too. Athletes train; bicyclists peddle; housewives and executives jog; children and dogs run.

If nothing else, it offers a convenient, measured test circle. How long does it take to walk 14,961.5 feet? Or 2.8336 miles?

For a get-acquainted lap, sunset is ideal, when pink clouds scamper over the sky and the sun drops behind houses on the west rim. Start anywhere: there are 14,961 choices. Parking areas are at East Green Lake Fieldhouse, at West Green Lake's old bathhouse, and the Aqua Theater at the south end. By car, drive Aurora Avenue north or south and follow signs to any of the above three points. By bus, take Stoneway Bus No. 6 at Third and Union for Aqua Theater or West Bathhouse, or Meridian Bus No. 16 (also at Third and Union) for East Fieldhouse.

The Aqua Theater holds pleasant memories for thousands of water shows and Broadway productions held on balmy summer nights since 1950. Turning north are green lawns under huge cottonwoods, alder, weeping willow, hawthorne, and swamp cypress. The path leaves East Green Lake Way, cuts across a ball field to the East Green Lake Fieldhouse, past rafts, diving boards, fishing pier, rental boats, and tennis courts on the north end. A stand of starched-white birch trees lines the northern path to the old West Green Lake Bathhouse, lately converted (swimmers nowadays arrive and leave in bathing suits) to a park theater and playhouse. Southward is the prettiest stretch. In spring, flowering crabs frame Mt. Rainier, across the water, like a Japanese print; masses of rhododendron and forsythia perfume the air under tall maples, larches, madronas, and birches. Ducks scurry across the grassy banks and into the water at your approach. Offshore, is Waldo Waterfowl Sanctuary, often called Swan Island or Duck Island and home to wildfowl—Muscovy, Peking ducks, coots, mal-

lards, and baldpate widgeons, the latter seen in great numbers during winter.

The name Green Lake appeared on a map as early as 1857. A big German, Green Lake John, settled a claim nearby about 1870. As the land developed, a trolley line was built. To get to the north shore from Seattle one rode two horsecar lines and two steamboats. Later, a car line ran from Fremont to the south shore and a steamboat ferried passengers across the lake.

Until recently, Green Lake was headed on the sorry path of all the hundreds of shallow Ice Age lakes in the Puget Sound country. "Fertilized" not only by natural nutrients but also by pollutants introduced by humanity, "coming into bloom" with algae, year by year the lake steadily became more unpleasant and even downright offensive. Many projects through the years attempted to clear the algae from Green Lake, which is only 15 feet deep. Now, however, the problem has been solved. Since 1962 some 3½ million gallons of clean mountain water have been pumped in every 24 hours, flushing out the nutrients. Green Lake has thus been saved.

Round trip 2.8 miles
Allow 1½ hours
Good all year
Dirt or paved path

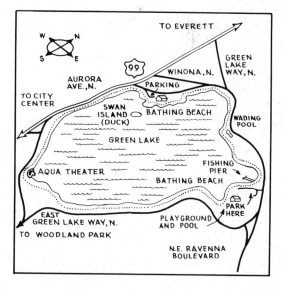

Early spring at Green Lake

2 COWEN AND RAVENNA PARKS

Little pockets of woodland beauty, tucked in the pleats of hilly Seattle, are like tiny Shangri-Las, known only to a select few who possess the curiosity to explore. Among the finest of these hideaways is a deep canyon north of the University District, divided, but only by name, into Cowen and Ravenna Parks. The ordinary park recreational features—ball field, tennis court, wading pool, etc.—are spread over the topside lawns of both Cowen and Ravenna, and often the

Trail in Ravenna Park

visitor has no hint he is missing the best part. To walk down into a mile-long canyon whose trees and foliage have been allowed to remain in a tangled natural state (with a little clearing and judicious extra planting) is like walking into the cellar of an abandoned house and finding it full of treasure.

The canyon can be reached from various points but for a start, drive north on Brooklyn Ave. NE or University Way to Cowen Park on NE Ravenna Boulevard. Park on side street nearby. (Or take any No. 7 bus on Third Avenue downtown and get off at Cowen Place.) Find the cinder path behind the old stone restroom building. It drops quickly under Cowen Park Bridge into the canyon—a new look at the tremendous arch supports of the complicated structure across which one casually rides so often. A path can be seen on the other side of the canyon also, which can be picked up and followed for variety on the return.

Once past the bridge and into the depths under dogwood and maples there is a muted cacophony of sounds heard all too seldom: birds by the hundreds protesting (or is it welcoming?) the advent of a stranger. The path, lined by tall European larches, reaches the floor of the canyon where fat squirrels play tag around tree trunks and a tiny creek, lathered thick with watercress, crosses the trail. About 2/3 mile is a junction with the trail seen earlier on the opposite side of the canyon. Under big California Redwood trees near the fork, a young mother sat quietly with her toddler on a recent summer outing, their glistening blond heads lifted to drink in the sounds of a world far apart from "up there."

A spring, channeled between cement troughs, drops to a rock-lined basin, flows under the path, out under ivy and watercress, and circles back again as though loath to leave. Deep under the watercress in the lowest reach of the gulch, an odd bubble pops lazily—one of the mineral springs that made Ravenna popular with the younger set of sailor-hat and balloon-sleeve days. (The mineral is sulphur and the water is no longer safe to drink.) Above the falls, the source of the stream is buried in a marsh of vitamin-green grass, stinging nettle, buttercup, and horsetail fern.

At the end the canyon opens to a level, play area. A paved path from there reaches the top of the bluff and playground area at the east end of Ravenna Park. Walk west across playfield and lawns and take one of the footpaths from the top down to the canyon floor to return to the car.

The gorge is an ice-age leftover, carved by the runoff from a huge glacial lake called Lake Russell by geologists. The waters draining into the ravine were diverted into underground channels when Lake Washington was lowered in building the Lake Washington Ship Canal. The rushing waters may have sought other channels, and the gorge they left behind may have caused many an engineer to curse when building the surrounding city. Nothing could be done with such a gorge but bridge it.

So it remains—a pocket of tranquil beauty.

Round trip 1.9 miles
Allow 1 hour
Good all year
Cinder path

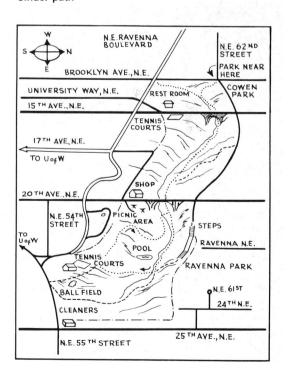

3   SALMON BAY

Two Seattle landmarks, Fisherman's Wharf and the Hiram M. Chittenden Locks, are so inextricably linked together they should be seen together. The latter confines and guards its "harem" of fishing boats in the wharf's snug seraglio and ushers them to and from the open sea, and the pageant of their procession is viewed by more than 2 million sightseers annually—mostly from the north side. This hike, south of Salmon Bay Waterway, shows the lesser-known, other side of the picture.

The Wharf is a fascinating sight all year. Seiners' nets are spread out for repair in June and gill netters come in before and after June. But winter is the ideal time for this hike. In January and February activity is at its height. Then the trollers, after a hard summer's work, are snubbed at their moorings and there is an air of controlled urgency as their owners paint, clean, saw, hammer, and immerse themselves in thick, gooey engines to be ready to leave about mid-March for another fishing season.

Drive to the south end of Ballard Bridge (15th Avenue West) and take exit west for Fisherman's Wharf (Emerson Street). Turn right at next street and park by a big sign with orientation map of the Wharf area. (By bus, take 15th Avnue N.W. No. 15, or Ballard No. 18 going north on First Avenue. Get off at Emerson Street and walk west four blocks to Wharf entrance.)

From the big sign, walk east toward Ballard Bridge past long net sheds. If a door is open, peek in for a look at a fisherman's tools. Gear for salmon-trolling, gill-netting, bottom-fish dragging, and halibut fishing are stacked high; floats in gay colors from egg-size plastics to football-size corks and huge marker buoys hang from locker walls and ceiling. Turn toward the water at the last street. Near the bridge, a boat or two may be up on the ways for repair or cleaning. Walk west along the dock and detour on one of the eight long piers for close-ups of the fishing armada. The piers can handle 600 vessels at a time, but up to 1500 come and go for a year's average.

Turn right past the restaurant, walk to the north end, go through a fence and gate on the left and continue west on Commodore Way. Views over Salmon Bay, the Canal Locks, and ship traffic between Puget Sound and Lake Washington are good company on this leg of a mile. At the Lockshore Apartments, 32nd Avenue West, find the sidewalk at the west end which leads downhill to the top of the spillway dam. Walk across the dam to the small locks. The surge of water from the 240-foot-long dam with its six gated openings will keep father busy answering questions. A fish ladder is at the south end. Cross the small locks when gates are closed; wait again for closing of the large lock gate and cross it to the north shore.

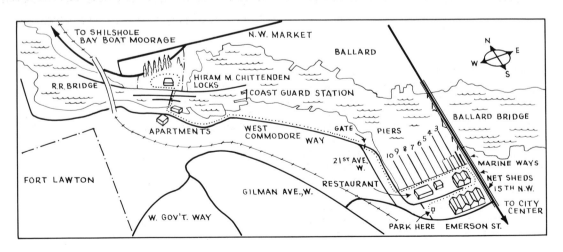

Oil tanker in the Hiram M. Chittenden Locks, Salmon Bay Waterway

At the administration building, pick up a descriptive brochure to help answer those bright-eyed questioners. Dates, construction details, purpose, and operation are detailed. Before leaving, walk through the 7 acres of botanic gardens on the slope behind the buildings, made lovely by imported trees and plants exchanged for Northwest ones by horticulturist Carl S. English, Jr. The gardens bring visiting botanists from many countries.

And YOUR out-of-town visitors who have experienced this hike can boast of their most unusual tour—a walk across the top of a canal.

Round trip 4.2 miles
Allow 2 hours (walk time only—
    browsing counts extra)
Good all year
Pavement and wooden docks

4 MARSHLAND TRAIL

Ever wished you could walk across water? Try the Arboretum Waterfront Nature Trail. This floating boardwalk skims across the marshland— a unique experience possible, so far, nowhere else in the country. The novelty has not worn off since completion of the trail in early 1968 and has drawn visitors from far places.

The water-walk is incorporated here as the first section of a 7½-mile one-way hike that extends from the Museum of History and Industry to Seward Park, from waterfront to waterfront. The four sections can be done separately as individual round trips or combined, as time and inclination allow. Any part offers scenic bonuses missed completely when sightseeing from a car.

Drive to the Museum of History and Industry, 2161 E. Hamlin Street. South of Montlake Bridge, enter Lake Washington Boulevard North and turn left immediately to the museum. (Or take Montlake Bus No. 4 going east on Pike Street. Get off at East Shelby Street and walk east to museum.) Park in the lot to the rear of the museum, at the lower level. The nature walk begins in the far east corner, at a concrete bridge. Crushed rock on a base of sawdust and wood chips is spread over cedar planks resting on Styrofoam floats.

Try a "shakedown cruise" to the left first. Follow the path under low trees, past tangled brush, along the ship canal and under Montlake Bridge ¼ mile, ending at the Seattle Yacht Club. Then return to the beginning and walk east. Spanning deep water, the deck walk seems to float off among reeds and rushes in an eye-pleasing series of angles. The University of Washington Stadium across the bay on the left is brutally large from this low viewpoint. The Evergreen Point Bridge approach, on the right, seems a monstrous concrete octopus flailing its arms above the marsh. But here, below the roar of traffic, is only the lap-lap of water against the floating deck-path . . . and avian parlor conversation.

Birds rule the tules here: they whish by overhead, land on swaying reeds, look straight at the stroller and chirp in his eye. Redwing blackbirds, swallows, sparrows, juncos, cowbirds, robins, varied thrushes, purple finches; the list is endless. Side-spurs wander into the reeds right or left, ending at concrete platforms where one can sit quietly among the inner rushes to watch coots, ducks, and perhaps (with luck) an occasional beaver or muskrat. Other spurs lead to canoe landing platforms jutting into Union Bay where one can dangle feet and watch boats chug-chug past, or glide silently under paddle or sail.

Joggers are encountered everywhere: they can be heard pounding the trail from afar—in time to move aside! A second concrete bridge, at about 1/3 mile, crosses deeper water, then the path turns left near open water and right again

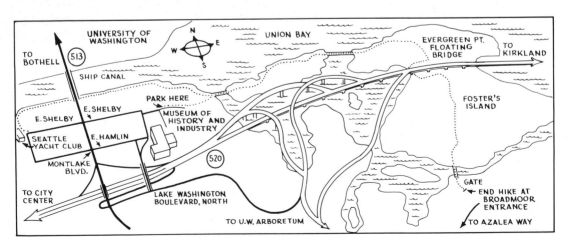

Nature trail in the Arboretum

shoreward to Foster's Island. Cross the greensward, perfumed by the heavy fragrance of delicate, cottony catkins on black cottonwoods in mid-April, or by the sweet balm of spirea in late May and June. Walk right on the intersecting path, up a slight incline to the bridge approach. An overpass is planned in future, but until it is built, follow the path under the highway span to the right. On the other side birches and big trees stand at attention along the wide path that crosses green lawns to a footbridge by the gate and iron fence enclosing residential Broadmoor.

For the next segment through the Arboretum, turn the page.

Round trip 2 miles
Allow 1¼ hours
Good all year
Floating dry-deck

5 ARBORETUM

Every Seattleite has his favorite season in the spacious University of Washington Arboretum. Early spring, with its flamboyant awakening of flowering cherries, flaming azalea bonfires, and platter-size rhododendrons must be seen to be believed. However, the metamorphosis of fall is every bit as glorious a pageant, and the one whose hues will be noted here.

As this revision goes to print, plans are under discussion to place all but 93.5 acres of the University of Washington's 200-acre Arboretum under state control and maintenance as a park. The inner core of scientific plantings may be restricted to vehicles, but walkers should still be welcome.

To do this segment of the Marshland-to-Seward Park hike separately, follow driving directions in preceding segment but continue south on Lake Washington Boulevard to the Arboretum's north entrance (Broadmoor) and park in area designated. (Or take Montlake Bus No. 4 to E. Lynn Street and walk east 3 blocks.)

Continue from the marshland nature trail which ends at the North Broadmoor entrance, go through the Arboretum gate past fishermen trying their luck on catfish, bass, crappies, and other "pan fish," and pick up Azalea Way across the paved main road, near the Arboretum offices and greenhouse. Ask there for a descriptive

folder on plants and flowering seasons.

The beginning of Azalea Way is marked by a sign and a big red cedar tree on the left. Signs identify most of the areas and varieties of plants. The path curves in a gentle descent between a stand of oaks (red, orange, and yellow) and graceful Japanese cherries.

In the Woodland Gardens are twin ponds studded with water lilies and rimmed by red-and-purple sweet gum trees, offset by the yellow and gold of nut trees—walnut, hickory, and pecan—farther south. Turn left at the lower pond and detour briefly through a cozy "valley" to the second pond (near the road). Here are gorgeous fall colors of 30 different types of Japanese maples, along with some white birches, one imported from China. Between the two ponds is a small picnic area, set in a colorful grove of dogwood and vine and Japanese maple, with banks of viburnum. Closer to the road above the second pond are warm hues of sourwood, witch hazel, and katsura trees. Return to Azalea Way. The Loderi Valley bordering the ponds has lost its radiant summer blooms, but the massed green banks still are elegant. Beyond them are scarlet-and-gold maples and the changeable-silk tones, golden yellow and silver, of ash, tamarack, larch, and birch.

At the foot of Rhododendron Glen, turn left past another pond and climb the slope among bronze-red serviceberry shrubs to a small hexagonal lookout. Then the climax: down the slope,

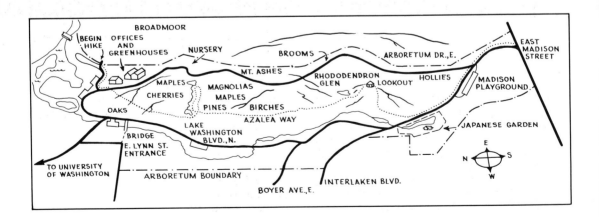

Stone lantern in Japanese Garden, University of Washington Arboretum

beyond a small parking lot at the end of Azalea Way, is the Japanese Garden, graced by delicate fronds of Japanese maples in reds and yellows. The garden, designed in Japan and constructed under supervision of Japanese landscape architects, is a pure delight.

From the Garden continue the walk along Lake Washington Boulevard to its junction with Arboretum Drive, marked by a small stone cot-tage, a charming old landmark. A few more steps uphill lead one to East Madison Street, to begin the next segment.

Round trip 2 miles
Allow 1 hour
Good all year
Grass-and-cinder path

6 LAKE WASHINGTON BOULEVARD NORTH

Summer has many attractions for a Lake Washington shore hike, wandering through arboreal residential areas and a succession of small parks. But the stroller will have company—plenty of it. Bathers crowd the beaches; traffic oozes like thick molasses along the boulevard. Come fall and a crisp snap to the air, the beaches are deserted, traffic sporadic, the foliage turns color and the hiker has the lake almost to himself.

The second segment of this four-part walk, along Azalea Way south through the Arboretum, ends at East Madison Street. Begin the third section by crossing Madison and heading southeast on Lake Washington Boulevard. The paved sidewalk ends soon after the intersection with East Mercer Street, but continue on the path beside the road, which bisects Lakeside Park and winds in two hairpin turns downhill to McGilvra Boulevard East. (The park, a small circle of 4½ acres, in autumn is an outdoor living room decorated with warm-hued scatter rugs—piles of fallen leaves—on its green floor. The manifold trunk of a huge alder tree in the center of the park looks like a tropical bamboo.)

Cross McGilvra and continue on Lake Washington Boulevard. Tiny Denny Blaine Park, a patch of green lawn with graceful birches and maples, is enclosed by a short loop drive dipping steeply from the boulevard to the shore. Farther south the autumn colors of Japanese maples, purple-leaved plum trees, and espaliered cotoneaster enfold mansions. The two-lane pavement descends slightly to an open shoreside strip with uncluttered views across blue waves to Cascade peaks. A row of pretty little cottages climbs into a cleft in the hillside north of the stub-end and bus-turnaround of Madrona Avenue.

Madrona Park, one of the oldest parks in the city, spreads south along the shore. Many of the big madronas for which the park was named are gone, but enough remain to carry the burden, along with weeping willows that feather-dust the roof of the former bathhouse, converted for youthful social activities (the modern swimmer arrives and leaves in his bathing suit). Homes become sparse, then numerous again where Lake

Washington Boulevard leaves the shore to go up the hillside. At the beginning of Lakeside Avenue South are a marina and stores. Above the forest of bobbing masts are the sloping green lawns of Leschi Park, where once Chief Leschi held camp "powwows"; a quiet pocket of tranquility still remains. The park is dominated by an 80-year-old giant sequoia planted by an early Park Department gardener. From here, on a clear day, Mount Baker can be added to the white Cascade cut-out that stretches south to Mount Rainier.

From Leschi Park the avenue narrows, passing shoreside mansions. The hike ends under the Lacey V. Murrow Bridge. South to Seward Park is another chapter in the lakeshore hike. For that, turn the page.

Round trip 5.3 miles
Allow 3 hours
Good all year
Pavement and dirt path

Sailboats racing on Lake Washington

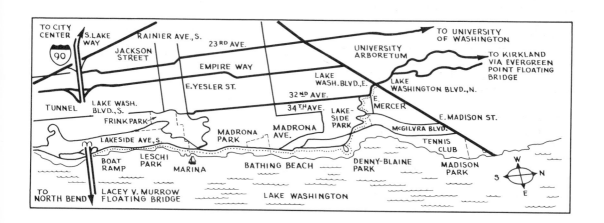

Sidewalk along Lake Washington Boulevard

7 LAKE WASHINGTON BOULEVARD SOUTH

Before starting this fourth and final leg, take a side-trip from Lakeside Avenue South down to one of the plazas beside the Lacey V. Murrow Bridge approach. From a nearly-private belvedere look out over the lake to Cascade peaks while the highway-maddened population swishes by with nary a glance up, down, or sidewise.

Getting from Seattle to and over Lake Washington was much more complicated in pioneer days, requiring a day's ride by horse through forest from Yesler's Mill on Elliott Bay, then hours of paddling by Indian canoe to the far shore.

South of the bridge the street reverts to its former name, Lake Washington Boulevard, now South. From here to Seward Park the shore strip is all city park. In 2 blocks is Colman Park, a 19-acre chunk of wooded land donated by J. M. Colman, Scotch sawmill king of the early 1900s. The seawall shows the former level of Lake Washington, which was lowered a half-century ago in one of man's first gross tinkerings, hereabouts, with the natural plan. Adjacent to Colman Park's south end is Mt. Baker Park. The shoreside parking lot is the site of an early water company installation pumping water to Seattle. The original little steam pump served to the point of heartbreak during the Great Fire of 1889, says

water historian Mary McWilliams. (Later, during the Alaska-Yukon-Pacific Exposition, Lake Washington "standby" water was accidentally pumped into city mains and killed dozens of citizens and an unknown number of visitors with typhoid fever.)

Just under 1 mile from Mt. Baker Park is Stanley Sayres Memorial Park, the center of activity during the annual "unlimited hydroplane" brawl. When quiet, the "pits" and nearby parking lot are a veritable Roman Forum of gabbing, quacking, waddling ducks and other waterfowl. A crust of bread from the pocket is a sure-fire bid for webbed-foot companionship.

Southward is the prettiest part of the lakeshore hike, with green lawns and lovely homes on the landward side and more webfoot company and views on the shore strip. The last mile is lined by a gift of Japanese cherry trees made to Seattle years ago by the city's Japanese residents. When in bloom the trees adorn the avenue with fragrant, flowering pink fountains—an appropriate approach to one of Seattle's loveliest parks—Seward Park. (Turn the page.)

Round trip 6.4 miles
Allow 3 hours
Good all year
Pavement and dirt path

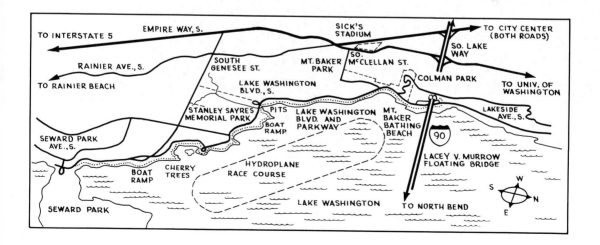

Forest in Seward Park

8   SEWARD PARK

Seward Peninsula, shaped like a mittened hand reaching from mainland into lake, offers a perfect woodland retreat—withdrawn from the madding crowd and traffic, yet easily accessible. This many-faceted gem of green, gold, and carmine hues stands offshore, the central treasure being a stand of old trees—one of only two virgin forests remaining in Seattle. Hard to believe; the same forest seen by Indians and the first settlers!

Enter Seward Park at Lake Washington Boulevard South and South Juneau Street and park near entrance. (By bus, take Rainier No. 7 going south on Third Avenue. Transfer at Rainier and Genesee to Seward Park shuttle bus No. 39.) Tucked within a small Japanese garden is a Taiko Gata lantern presented to Seattle by Yokohama citizens in gratitude for our assistance in their earthquake of 1923. A Japanese torii, or gateway, lends simple elegance to the green lawn nearby. The tall lacquered structure, held together by hardwood pins, is also a gift to the city by our Japanese residents, duplicating a torii on a sacred Japanese isle.

From the torii, walk the wooded path uphill to a picnic area under tall firs and maples. Andrews Bay, seen between mainland and peninsula, was named for an early homesteader and Park Board Commissioner. Here the paved road splits around the amphitheater, the two segments joining in ½ mile. Follow the left branch .2 mile to the parking area above the amphitheater, a spacious lawn where summer concerts are held overlooking the lake. A few feet beyond, find a wide, needled forest path left of the road. The path entrance, barred to auto traffic, begins a ¾-mile forest hike straight through the center of the peninsula. From the north end, hike back to the car along either the east or west beach. An extra treat on the east side is a visit to a game fish hatchery, where thousands of fingerlings are bred.

Where the trail begins, tall Lombardy poplars become a massive bonfire when struck by the sun. Deeper in the woods, a conglomerate of towering Douglas firs, cedars, hemlocks, spruce, big-leaf maple, and alder shade and nourish a ground cover of ferns and salal—Seattle's forest primeval. About halfway, the trail branches through a meadow; the two variants unite at the end, where the path drops to picnic tables, restroom, and beach. Views here across water east to Mercer Island, north to the floating bridges, and west to the mainland.

The area was purchased for a park in 1911 and named in honor of William H. Seward, known for his part in purchasing Alaska.

Round trip 3.8 miles
Allow 2½ hours
Good all year
Road and forest path

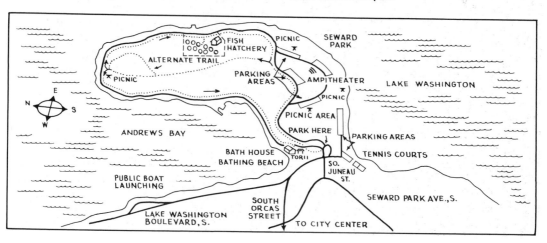

9   SCHMITZ PARK

Because someone cared, Seattle still has a tract where one can walk through virgin forests that have changed little from the days before "civilization" crept over the land. The first thing on our agenda for out-of-town visitors is a trip to Alki Point and an explanation of the pioneer landing site. From there, a few blocks away, they are shown the forest as it looked to the first arrivals—sans paved streets, row on row of homes, apartment buildings, stores, and eateries. Schmitz and Seward Parks are the only two areas in Seattle where one can stand under trees, look up a trunk rising straight as a ruler 100 feet or more into the sky and think: "So this is the way it was!" Pioneers Ferdinand and Emma Schmitz

Schmitz Park

must have seen far ahead of their time, for they began the park with a gift to the city of 23 acres in 1908, provided it would be preserved forever with no change, as a reminder of the forests in which they homesteaded. Additional pieces were added from time to time by various donors to bring the park acreage to a total of 50.4 acres.

Drive west on S.W. Admiral Way to the entrance marked by a large sign at S.W. Stevens Street. (By bus, take West Seattle-Alki No. 15 going south on First Avenue and get off at park entrance.) Follow the road down into a canyon and park in the lot provided. Begin the walk on an uphill trail to the right of a gully south of the parking lot. Trails wind all through this area; the hiker may explore and find his own favorites, but for now, this get-acquainted loop route will give basic orientation.

Fat-boled trees, some 8 feet in diameter, are an immediate escort. Shortly a faint trail appears to the left. Ignore it for another on the left a few feet beyond—a digression from the main trail, but too pleasant to skip. Over log-braced steps, through patches of skunk cabbage and wildflowers, it climbs slightly to a tiny green plateau that forms a perfect picnic spot. Beside a huge stump with axe marks, a big cedar, gutted by fire, still clings to life. If the ground is dry, sprawl against the jutting roots of another tall tree and listen awhile to the birds. Then return to the main trail and continue up the gully. In less than $1/4$ mile take a right branch that diverges from the trail. (The left leads to a junction and a return trail for a shorter loop hike.) The dappled, sunlit path climbs higher above the gully, scrambled with mountainous logs and stumps swathed in green velvet moss and tangled with vines and ferns.

At about $1/2$ mile the trail forks again. Take the left which crosses the head of the stream. (The right leads to overgrown log steps that climb the remaining 100-foot slope to residences on S.W. Manning Street.) On the opposite side of the stream, the path doubles back to the junction with the shorter loop. From there, follow one of two trails straight ahead (a third one on the right leads to S.W. Hinds Street). Either path skirts above the gully back to the parking lot. The second time around, vary the route by following

the shorter loop and other paths. The feeling of the wilderness will not pall, thanks to our thoughtful friends, Emma and Ferdinand Schmitz!

Round trip 1 mile (once around)
Allow 1 hour
Good all year
Dirt forest path

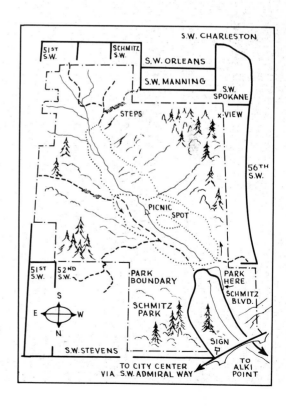

10   ALKI BEACH

To a newcomer from a landlocked area, our uncounted miles of saltwater beach around inlets, bays, and islands add up to a special kind of hiker's Valhalla. We tend to take them for granted, but thankfully they are always there, ready for our whims. Ever have that whim in winter?

If not, it is a privilege too casually discarded. Few areas in our country have beaches pleasant in winter, with variable moods of water and sky for exhilarating walks. From October on, when the air turns nippy, the crowds are gone. One can stroll the beaches for miles with only gulls and waterfowl for company. Try an early dawn hike on a crisp, clear day, when the water is choppy and gunmetal gray, the Olympic and Cascade ranges sharp and white and hard. Or for a restful night's sleep, hike at dusk when the same stark mountain ranges are softened with the magenta glow of the setting sun. At our Vashon Island beach home years ago, our only heat came from driftwood, and often we rose

Lighthouse on Alki Point

before dawn to gather a thick bark bonanza before the ebb tide carried it away again. Our memories now? Not aching backs, but glorious winter dawns we would otherwise have missed.

For a start, try a beach close to home. Alki is a favorite because one cannot be trapped by high tide, not with the sidewalk alongside. Drive on Alki Beach Drive to Alki Point Lighthouse and park by the gate. (By bus, take West Seattle-Alki No. 15, get off at 63rd Avenue S.W. and Alki Beach Drive and walk west 4 blocks to the lighthouse.)

Within daytime visiting hours posted, first tour the lighthouse, one of Puget Sound's oldest and most interesting. It dates from the first kerosene lantern hung on a pole in the 1870s by Hans Martin Hanson out of consideration for mariners. From the station, walk east on Alki Drive 2 blocks to 65th Avenue S.W. where the seawall marks the city park boundary. (Hikers often round the point in front of the lighthouse at low tide, which is permissible; but crossing a short strip of private property sandwiched between city and lighthouse land is subject to owner's permission.) The monument at 63rd Avenue S.W., bearing the names of the first settlers who landed here from the schooner **Exact**, marks probably the most hallowed site in the city. Picture their stepping on the barren, sand-and-rock beach backed by forest giants that dripped continually that gray, rainy, November day, 118 years ago. New York Alki, "New York by and by," they called it. The miracle of faith.

Another monument, a replica of the Statue of Liberty erected by Boy Scouts of America, is at 61st Avenue S.W. Beyond is a 2-mile stretch of beach, wide and free to Duwamish Head. Just around the Head is a tiny green picnic spot decorated by a huge, rusty anchor. From here is a fine cityscape across Elliott Bay, from Magnolia Bluff past Seattle Center and the Space Needle, south to Harbor Island.

From New York to Seattle Alki.

Round trip 4 miles
Allow 3 hours (to include lighthouse tour)
Good all year
Rocky or sandy beach, depending on tide

Anchor recovered from the bay, Alki Beach

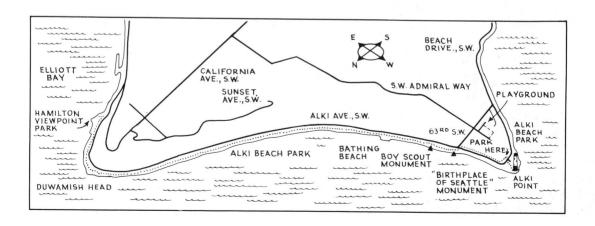

39

11   LINCOLN PARK

One visit to Lincoln Park is like eating one peanut. Not enough. Sample this large and lovely West Seattle park, just north of the Fauntleroy ferry dock, and you'll return often.

With spring's first sun the grass warms and Seattleites flock to loll on the greensward, to stretch uninhibited, to release the pressures of a gray, damp winter, to stroll for miles on the beach, to walk or bicycle through woods or meadow or over expansive lawns, to sit and dream at splendid views and sunsets over mountains and sea. This magnificent 130-acre park has all this, plus playground, tennis court, picnic areas with stoves, and a public swimming pool.

For a first "acquaintance tour," go to the south parking lot off Fauntleroy Avenue opposite S.W. Cloverdale St. (By City Transit bus take Fauntleroy (Lincoln Park) No. 18, going south on First Avenue.) On succeeding trips, try other entrances and parking areas.

In springtime, the entrance is a carpet of daisies on a lush green lawn accented by flowering cherries under tall cedars and firs. Follow the path that leads, in 5 minutes, directly to the beach by a paved ramp. Above the roof of an open kitchen with wood ranges and tables, you may witness a crow caucus, sitting by twos on the limbs of a dead fir. As if by signal they set up a chorus—CAW! CAW!

Walk the beach along the seawall clear to the north end of the park, nearly a mile; some sand, some rocks, but easy and one of the nicest beach walks in the city. The park is shaped like a triangle, and Williams Point, named during the 1841 Wilkes Expedition, forms the apex where Colman Pool and Bathhouse (salt water) stands. The pool is open to the public from school closing to school opening.

Behind the pool a wide path leads to the top—much easier and safer than two others near the path's north terminus, which are steep, eroded and dangerously slippery. All return to the bluff edge, thence back to the starting point. Superb views of Sound, islands, and Olympic Mountains on one side; on the other, the landscaping. Azaleas and rhododendrons set off small bonfires under cedar, dogwood, hemlock, fir, alder, and maple, then comes an unusual grove of madronas.

A particularly interesting tree is a Chinese "Golden Rain" near the wading pool by the street at the north end. It grew from a shoot from Indiana planted by Lieutenant George Davidson, who, on a surveying brig in 1857, astutely named the cove Fauntleroy for his father-in-law to be.

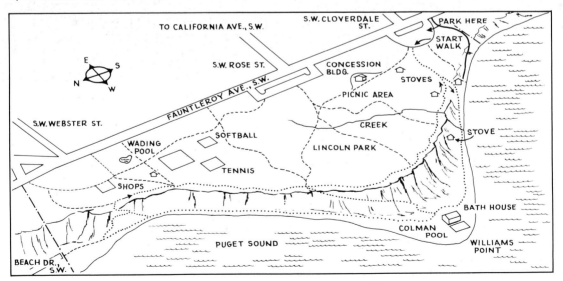

Puget Sound and Olympic Mountains from Lincoln Park

Davidson further advanced his courtship by immortalizing his future family along the lofty Olympic horizon. The highest peak seen from Seattle he called Constance, for the sister of his fiance, Ellinor, whose name he placed on a more delicate mountain on the far south. The double-summited peak between he named The Brothers for the two Fauntleroy boys.

The city bought the land in 1923 for the purpose of erecting a statue in a major park named for our 16th President. The park does

justice to his name, even though the statue never materialized.

Round trip 2 miles
Allow 1½ hours
Good all year
Beach party paved, partly rocky; dirt path in park

12   INDIAN TRAIL

Seattle has many delights for the resident planning his dream home. He can find any type of terrain or scenic setting he wants—hilltop or valley; salt water shore or sweet; forest or field. And by the same token, endless opportunities of views and terrain for the hiker. Where he goes, the residential atmosphere changes with the terrain.

When out-of-town guests ask to see various living modes here, try them on the "Indian Trail." Something about the setting—the charm and atmosphere of homes hanging piggy-back on the hillside above Three Tree Point—is as quaintly distinctive as a chiaroscuro treatment of picturesque Old Town in Lisbon, Portugal.

Drive to Burien, turn west on SW 152nd Street to the end, then south as it becomes Maplewild Avenue SW and winds parallel to shore. Just before reaching Three Tree Point, turn right on first street (SW 170th St.) past Three Tree Point Grocery. (If car is not available take Des Moines bus routed through Seahurst. Get off at the grocery.) Continue past junction with Three Tree Point Lane and park out of way near dead end at beach. Look for steps to the public path at the rear of the last house on the right. The path is maintained as an easement for residents and is somewhat like an old-fashioned back alley, threading between fences of homes on the hill above, on the right, and sliding down to seashore on the left, all with individual footpaths linked to the "Indian Trail."

Every architectural style is represented — formal, rustic, modern, some almost Victorian. Even fences bear the stamp of individuality; rustic rails, white-painted picket, laurel, holly, privet. Fences wreathed with roses, sweet peas, phlox, dahlias. Names are "written" in rope, nail studs, cut wood, or metal. Boats from Tom Thumb size to yachts ride the waves offshore, and glimpses are seen over them of the Olympics, beyond the wakes of ferries, freighters, and small boats traced on the blue waters. The trail climbs higher above the shoreline under an arch of tall trees, and berry vines now fight to reclaim cultivated lawns and gardens. Suddenly the path comes out on a circular driveway. But it does not end. Walk across the lower end of the loop and pick up the trail again on the far side. It continues between more fences beside intriguing lawns that look years older. Four tall fir trees here appear to be almost strangled with ivy, so completely covered from base to top they look like props for a Mars scenario. Beyond the tall trees the path is walled by thick laurel on one side, banks of salal and berry vines on the other, then all too soon, the path ends on the pavement of Maplewild Avenue.

Old-timers say it has been called the Indian Trail ever since the white man came to settle. Be-

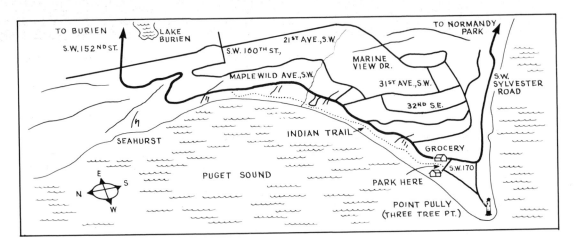

Houses built on steep hillside along the Indian Trail at Three Tree Point

fore that, Indians followed the shoreline route this path takes around the point. It continued many more miles. Traces in other parts can be followed, where known. Point Pully, as it still appears on marine maps, was named by the Wilkes Expedition in 1841 for Robert Pully, quartermaster in the crew. But early residents quickly adopted Three Tree Point for three tall trees near the point. Recently a garden club replaced the old trees with three new ones, in deference to boating fans who missed the handy landmark of old.

Round trip 1-2/3 miles
Allow 1 hour
Good all year
Dirt path

13   SALTWATER STATE PARK

"Go back to Illinois?" a new settler repeated the question in astonishment. "When I can go picnicking 10 minutes after I get home from work? Not a chance."

Because of its location and varied attractions Saltwater State Park has grown in popularity and looks since depression days of the 1930s when the Civilian Conservation Corps cleared the park and built a seawall and community kitchens. Now it draws thousands each year to its picnic tables and overnight campsites. Many a Girl or Boy Scout, Campfire or Rainbow girl has fond memories of group camp-outs on the hill above a gurgling brook. If possible, go on a week day, especially in summer. Weekends are crowded.

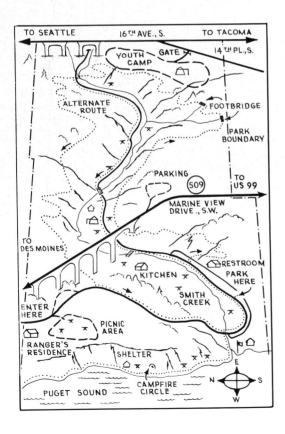

From September on, there is room to move. Winter days are often ideal.

Drive Interstate 5 or Highway 99 to Kent-Des Moines exit, turn west on State 516 and south at junction with 509 in Des Moines. In 1½ miles the park road branches right, marked by a sign, and drops steeply to a parking area by the beach. To go by bus, take suburban Des Moines-Zenith (irregular schedule—call for information) to the park entrance.

Two miles of trails wind through woods on the hill above the beach. The beach strip is pleasant walking, but one can only go 1200 feet. Beyond park boundary the hiker trespasses on private land; otherwise he could hike all the way north to Des Moines. Try the beach strip first, then find the forest trail to the left of the restroom. It spirals up the steep slope in easy switchbacks. The path, almost ankle-deep in leaves in fall, rises above the gully and passes under the south end of a high concrete bridge on Marine View Drive. The sun shining through tall maples and alders makes a shadow filigree of vines and ferns over fallen logs; salal and Oregon grape hide shy trilliums and bunchberry. The trail reaches what seems the head of a draw and crosses a log footbridge (constructed by the CCC in 1935) spanning a musical waterfall that drops in natural terraces choked with brush and fallen logs. Across the bridge and around a curve is another footbridge over a trilling rillet. The path becomes narrower, descends round the hillside past a youth camp area, then climbs again to an intersection of sorts. The lower branch to left, more overgrown, drops quickly to the valley floor and a paved road beside Smith Creek. Go straight instead, across the wide swath to the right (it leads to hilltop residences) 700 yards farther downhill to a fork above the same paved road. Go left (the right again leads to residences on 16th Street) and walk west on the road about 100 feet to another small footbridge.

From here, one can return to the parking lot by the paved road following the creek through the canyon, past more campsites and picnic tables. Or cross the footbridge and continue the trail over two more stream crossings and partway up the opposite canyon wall. It turns west to the north end of the bridge and parking lot opposite

Trail above campground, Saltwater State Park

the ranger's residence. Return to the car by the road. This adds another 1/5 mile to the round-trip total given below, but keeps the hiker in the woods longer. And away from people! There were 670,000 in the park in 1968. Most of them stayed on the road and beach.

Round trip 3 miles
Allow 2 hours
Good all year
Forest path and paved road

Puget Sound from Samish Island quarry

14 SAMISH ISLAND

The name is misleading: Samish Island no longer is an island. Early settlers put on boots at low tide and slushed across the ooze of tide flats to the mainland, but now the slough is filled in and the traveler is not aware the peninsula he approaches once was surrounded by water. The "island" does retain the isolated beauty of sea views from high bluffs, lovely homes, beaches. There is also the poignancy of history: of visiting Indians who gathered to dig clams; of resident Indians who lived in a long-house; of pioneers who rowed from the beach to side-wheel steamers anchored offshore; of bull-team logging days and the odor of dogfish being rendered on the beach for oil to lubricate the skids. All nostalgic memories now. But the makings of a beautiful walk.

Drive Interstate 5 to Burlington exit, thence northwest on State 11 to Edison. Go through the settlement; the way jogs left, then right again on Samish Island highway, which meanders 4 miles across flat farmland. At a sign announcing arrival on the island, the highway turns left and climbs to the top of a bluff overlooking Padilla Bay. Pass a large filbert plantation and less than 1 mile farther is an intersection. Turn left, uphill again. Cottages line the drive, all so individual each one commands attention: stone cottages in a setting of madronas; a log cabin among trees grown over with ivy. The road continues another ½ mile to the Samish Island Fire Department Station.

Park out of the way near station and begin the hike straight ahead, along the bluff edge overlooking the bay. The road makes a sharp right turn at a girls' camp entrance gate. Turn right with the road and continue until a cable, strung between a big cedar and a hemlock, blocks the road. Beyond the chain it is about 1/6 mile to the shore. The private owner has given permission to walk, pending a change in status. If signs are posted against trespassing, respect them.

Beyond the chain barrier, the road fades into a grassy track that passes old farm buildings and ends at the bluff overlooking the Strait of Georgia. Facing the water all the way to the edge, the stroller is unaware of his unusual surroundings. When he turns away from the sea, he finds himself in a sunken bowl formed by the high wall of an old rock quarry. The effect is somewhat like an outdoor amphitheater—a private one. Try an oration! The quarry was the source for years of large boulders used for fill-ins, ballast, and shoring. Much of it was used to change the island to a peninsula. To the right is William Point. Somewhere along this shore, it is said, rumrunners established a base during Prohibition days. Tradition has it that the Samish Indian chief lived near William Point; later, a mailboat brought letters from the mainland for all the outer islands.

From the chain barrier, turn left on the first paved road to return to the car at the store. This stretch forms the third side of the triangular walk, allowing still different views of homes and island life.

Round trip 2-1/3 miles
Allow 2 hours
Good all year
Road and grass-grown track

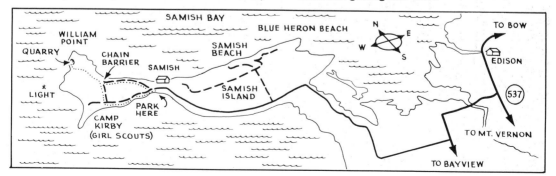

15   BAY VIEW STATE PARK

Lying in the lush lowlands of Skagit Flat, this lovely park has a saltwater beach on protected Padilla Bay; from the 100 campsites, sunsets swirl like flaming capes over San Juan Islands to the west.

Drive north on Interstate 5 through Mount Vernon and take the Anacortes Highway (State 536) west for 6 miles. Turn north on Bayview-Edison Road 3 miles to park entrance.

At present, the campsite areas are all on the east side of the highway, set among tall cedars and Douglas firs, with the beach across the road. Since first publishing, two small acquisitions of land have added 400 feet or more to the former beach, and a new bathhouse is in future plans. A new highway underpass also has been added, allowing easy passage to and from the upper park level and the beach area, with parking lots at both levels.

Drive first to the upper level picnic and campground area. Park in marked area near kitchen and rest rooms. Walk the road uphill from there to an open field (being modernized at this writing for campground) surrounded by woods. Radiating from this field are several overlapping dirt lanes. Begin your woods hike anywhere and wend among enticing campsites under tall trees. Each loop returns to the field; all in all they total about a mile. Follow up the trails with a stroll on the beach: take the underpass below the highway. Picnic tables have been added to the newly improved beach area, offering a choice between arboreal or salt-air munching. Warm, saltwater swimming on a sandy beach is available.

Even before you set foot on the rock-and-pebble shore, invigorating sea air tumbles over you in breakers. The smell of the sea is in a class with the fragrance of pine forests; neither can be synthesized.

Roughly 1/2 mile of beach within park boundaries is legally yours to enjoy. (Many have hiked several miles farther north, but private property is crossed and we caution against trespassing. Ask the park ranger about possible restrictions first.)

All the while there are views: the Olympic Mountains west; Guemes Island beyond March Point northwest, hazy in smoke from refineries near Anacortes; a hump of Cypress Island beyond Guemes; and tall on the horizon, Mount Constitution on Orcas Island.

Round trip 2 miles, woods and beach
Allow 2 hours
Good anytime
Dirt lane and sandy beach

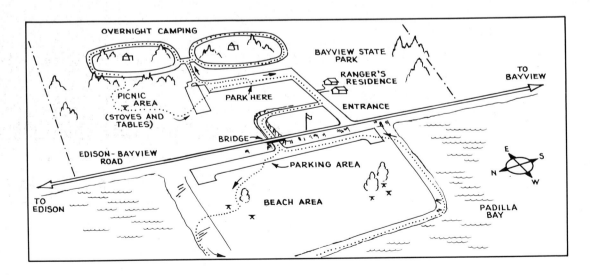

Padilla Bay from Bay View State Park

16 WASHINGTON PARK

Good old Tonges H. Havekost may not have guessed at the earth-moving changes that would come after his passing, but whatever his reasons for preserving his chosen corner of the world for the public to enjoy, time has compounded the interest on our indebtedness to him. On this easy 2.8-mile loop around Fidalgo Head, the views are spectacular and varied. Take a picnic lunch—this park offers endless invitations to satisfy esthetic as well as physical hunger.

In Anacortes, follow signs for Victoria ferry.

Mount Erie from Washington Park

Continue on the main road past the dock entrance 2 miles to Washington Park. To right of the entrance is Sunset Beach picnic area, if lunch is in order first. Go left to parking area. Leave the car and begin hike on one-lane dirt road, marked "Scenic Route," to the right of the restroom.

Views are immediate and constant: Decatur and Lopez Islands, nearest across Rosario Strait; San Juan Island behind them; and dimly seen across Haro Strait beyond, Victoria, B.C. Halfway to the first bend in the road is a Douglas fir "freak." Traditionally the species grows straight as a rocket lift in the forest, but this one grew almost horizontally from the bluff and stretches almost 70 feet over the rocky shore, as if longing to take a saltwater dip.

The road bends left at West Beach, where a path leads down about 25 feet to the sandy shore of a snug little cove popular with skindivers. The road climbs gradually through heavy forest and doubles in one switchback before reaching Juniper Point and the summit of Fidalgo Head. Here is a stand of 200-year-old juniper trees — mere seedlings when Captain George Vancouver sailed by on his voyage of discovery. Vancouver noted similar trees he thought were cypress on a nearby island, which he named for them.

A gnarled, wind-tortured patriarch bearing only a few clumps of foliage still stubbornly stands guard on the point overlooking Burrows Bay and Burrows Island. One can't blame the tree for hanging on; the views are endless. An expanse of blue waters and green headlands reaches as far as eyes can see. One can even pick out Deception Pass Bridge, Fidalgo's link to Whidbey Island. A picnic table here is a good halfway rest stop on the hike.

About .1 mile beyond the picnic table, to the right of the road downhill, is a monument to Havekost. Across the road, opposite, is a remarkable reservoir formed of natural granite boulders. Rock outcroppings and boulders with scuff marks of glaciers cover the ground between here and the monument.

Havekost, a pioneer of 1871, owned much of the land around Flounder Bay, which his monument overlooks (originally named Boxer Bay by Charles Wilkes). He bequeathed a portion of Fidalgo Head to the City of Anacortes with the provision that the land be used as a park. Flounder Bay changed contours markedly after Havekost's death in 1910. A mill and a long dock were constructed on pilings. Flounder Bay, which served as the millpond, was dredged for shipping channels and filled on its west side for buildings. For 30 years the mill supported 150 men and a hotel, railroad station, and recreation hall. The mill was demolished in 1961; an airfield occupies the fill area and the planing mill, the size of two football fields, is used as a boat storage building near the Skyline Marine Dock and Restaurant.

At least, Havekost saved for us Fidalgo Head and its views.

Round trip 2.8 miles
Allow 2 hours
Good all year
Dirt lane

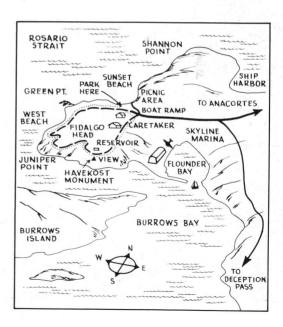

17   MOUNT ERIE

In 1841 the U.S. Navy explorer of Puget Sound, Lieutenant Charles Wilkes, honored Commodore Oliver Hazard Perry by naming "Perry Island." That didn't stick; it is now Fidalgo Island. Wilkes also called the island's high peak "Erie" after Perry's victorious Battle of Lake Erie. That stuck. But don't be surprised if Mount Erie someday becomes Mount Auld. To local folk, Ray Auld is much more deserving of being identified with their beautiful hill than is a minor battle in an ignominious war fought far away from Puget Sound country.

To find the mountain, enter Anacortes on State 536 and drive to 32nd Avenue, turn left at sign for Mount Erie and left again (south) on H Street. Residences recede as the road ascends gradually through woods and bursts out beside lovely, lily-bordered Heart Lake, about 2 miles from town. Watch here for a small sign, "Ray Auld Drive." Turn left into a wide level area behind trees and bushes and park. A sign for Mount

Campbell Lake and Skagit Bay from Mount Erie

Erie, invisible from the highway, now is seen. (Ray Auld Drive parallels the highway a short distance. Its south end is more clearly marked "Mount Erie" for northbound travelers.)

Begin hike on paved Auld Drive, ascending gradually south, then steeply around the base of Sugar Loaf Mountain. In about 1 mile the road makes a wide, hairpin curve and climbs steeply west another mile to Erie's crest. The unused radar installation buildings just before the summit parking lot are a relic of a military boondoggle of the 1950s.

To reach view platforms, walk from the summit parking lot on glacier-polished slabs down steps to a cement platform, with sturdy iron rail, built out on the glacier-plucked cliff. Superb views east (over tops of firs rooted 100 feet below) of snowy Cascades from Garibaldi in Canada south to Rainier on the horizon, and in the foreground, endless bays, inlets, and islands. Take along a map and try to sort them out: past Anacortes refineries to smaller Hat Island and larger Guemes Island; March Point jutting into Padilla Bay; Similk Bay south, with its tiny islands, Hope and Skagit. Behind the radar building is another viewing platform. At toetip is Campbell Lake, with its own tiny island—an idyllic children's playground—and beyond, Pass Lake and Lake Erie to the west. On cliffs below this platform, students in The Mountaineers Climbing Course practice rock-climbing techniques.

In 1951, the Kiwanis Club donated to the City of Anacortes Park Department 150 acres of land including the entire summit and adjacent area. Additional donations extend the city's park area surrounding Little Cranberry Lake to a total of 450 acres for use as park property only.

The hill is beautiful because Ray Auld saw to it. A "magnicent obsession" to make it the most beautiful road in the country, the project—7 miles of road—took him 20 years. While this edition was going to press, he passed away at the age of 88, right after working on his beloved road. Certainly we can drive up quickly and lazily; but by walking we can appreciate his contribution. With "paint brushes" of ax, brush hook, rake, and spade, he cleared jumbles of deadfall, planted vine maple for fall color, and dogwood and rhododendrons under towering Douglas firs, and transplanted pink water lilies in the lake beside the road.

If Nature took hundreds of years to create towering firs, Auld explained, he could spare time to help with the background. Obviously, he never sat around asking: "What can I do?"

Round trip 4 miles
Allow 3 hours
High point 1300 feet
Elevation gain 1200 feet
Good all year
Paved road

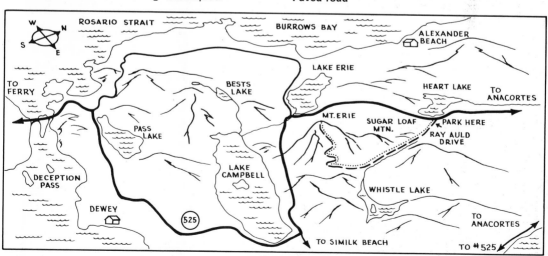

18   EBEY'S LANDING

Stand on the lonely, windswept bluff marked by a small, bleak monument and look across Admiralty Inlet to Port Townsend, where ocean liners can be seen heading out to sea. How often did Colonel Isaac Ebey, 116 years ago, do the same? Somehow this spot, Ebey's Landing, retains a mournful sadness. Ebey was a man of courage, with a dedicated past and a bright future. His bad luck was the Haida Indians, who selected him as a target for revenge, murdered and beheaded him at the front door of his home, while family and friends fled from the rear door.

Drive north on US 525 from ferry dock on Whidbey Island 28 miles, turn southwest on Ebey Road (next road north of Coupeville exit), and follow signs for Ebey's Landing. The solitary monument bearing a simple inscription is on the edge of the bluff to the left just before the road drops the last 25 feet to the beach. Park there and begin hike going north. Caution: Time the hike to start with ebb tide; at certain points it is easy to be trapped by incoming tide against the cliff, especially during a storm. Take picnic lunch and carry water. A wonderful season is early spring, when marsh grass and wildflowers bend in the breeze near the lagoons.

Before leaving Ebey's Landing, take note of

Old blockhouse near Ebey's Landing

the bluff above the beach. A trail there is an alternate for the return. It skirts the edge by a farmer's field, recedes deeply around the end of a gorge, and fans seaward again to the highest viewpoint of the hike, with spectacular views from Mount Baker east to the Olympics west. A long, dry lagoon (actually a tidal backwash) at the north end of the bluff is a good marker to watch for on the return. From it is a gradual climb from beach to the blufftop.

Just before reaching Partridge Point, 4 miles from the Landing monument and near where a private road dips to beach homes, are ruined pill-boxes hanging from the cliff, but for how long? The wind stirs and pebbles cascade from underneath. Behind them is tiny Lake Pondilla, cradled in a tree-lined hollow.

This is the old Fort Ebey, built for coastal defense and waiting funds for development as a state park. Until then, entry within the fort area is prohibited—in fact, hazardous. Missing manhole covers of old bunkers could result in dangerous falls into dark passages below. End your hike with a picnic lunch at Partridge Point, where Libbey Road drops to a wide landing cut into the bluff.

Colonel Ebey, for whom the fort was named, traveled cross-country from Missouri in 1848, joined in the California gold rush, then came to Puget Sound. In 1850 he explored much of King County by Indian canoe, the first white man to go into its interior. He filed claim and settled on a farm on Whidbey Island. In 7 years he commanded volunteer troops in Indian wars, worked as deputy collector of customs, was a member of the Oregon Legislature, pushed for establishing a separate Washington Territory, and set his sights for a higher office—even Governor.

For a final interesting landmark, drive from Ebey's Landing to the pioneer cemetery high on a hill (follow the map) where a blockhouse built in Ebey's day still remains among the graves of many early settlers, enclosed in quaint picket or rusty iron fences.

Round trip 8 miles
Allow 5 hours
Good all year; best in spring
Rocky beach and dirt paths

Strait of Juan de Fuca from Ebey's Landing on Whidbey Island

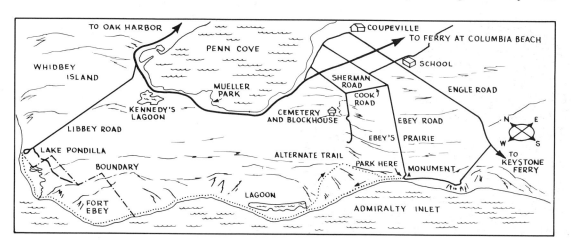

TO OAK HARBOR

PENN COVE

COUPEVILLE
TO FERRY AT COLUMBIA BEACH

WHIDBEY ISLAND

MUELLER PARK

SCHOOL

SHERMAN ROAD

ENGLE ROAD

KENNEDY'S LAGOON

COOK ROAD

LIBBEY ROAD

CEMETERY AND BLOCKHOUSE

EBEY ROAD

N
E
W
S

LAKE PONDILLA

EBEY'S PRAIRIE

ALTERNATE TRAIL

TO KEYSTONE FERRY

BOUNDARY

PARK HERE

MONUMENT

FORT EBEY

LAGOON

ADMIRALTY INLET

19   FORT CASEY

The long, gray days of Puget Sound winter and four-square confinement getting you down? Hie thee and thine hence to Fort Casey. Whatever the season, few places offer so ideal a petcock to let off steam. The young ones can run their legs off on wide-open, grassy lawns sloping to the sea, over concrete gun emplacements, and in and up the circular staircase of a quaint little lighthouse. Liberal spoonsful of history painlessly ingested with the whipped cream of joyous physical liberation. Take a picnic lunch—water is provided in a picnic area.

Drive Interstate 5 to Mukilteo exit and ferry to Whidbey Island. Or drive south by land from Anacortes. From ferry dock go north on State 525, turn left (west) on State 113 and follow signs past Keystone ferry, then left at next two junctions. From Anacortes, drive south, then west on Ebey Road. The entrance road splits north of the Keystone Ferry dock and climbs uphill, approaching fort grounds from the rear and over the top of old mortar bunkers. At the top is the picnic area. Note it mentally for later and continue downhill to parking lot below ranger's residence.

The fort grounds are open all year, 8 to 5 p.m., but the Interpretive Center at the lighthouse is open only April 1 to September 30 (plus a few weekends and holidays in the remainder of the year). Exhibits in the lighthouse, however, trace the area's history from Spanish-American War days and help immensely to understand the fort's construction.

So begin the hike with the lighthouse, north of the parking lot. Beginning service in 1861, it marked Admiralty Head and guided ships into Admiralty Inlet. The present building replaced the older in 1899, but the light was decommissioned before the fort was declared surplus in 1954. Now walk down the jeep road below the lighthouse to the Van Horne gun battery at the north boundary of the state park site. (Buildings on shore below are barracks of Camp Casey, Seattle Pacific College property.) Find the path on shoreward side of the gun battery and follow it south along the top of the bluff through rippling waves of marsh grass, dock, and wild margaritas until it reaches the north end of the main line of gun emplacements. Climb the steps inside the first one marked Worth (batteries are named for war veterans, mostly Spanish-American). In this is a clear example of the oldest (1898) and newest (1907) cement poured, side by side. Walk the length of the bunkers, topside or below, to the far end.

Fort Casey's guns were never "fired in anger," as contemporary historians quaintly put

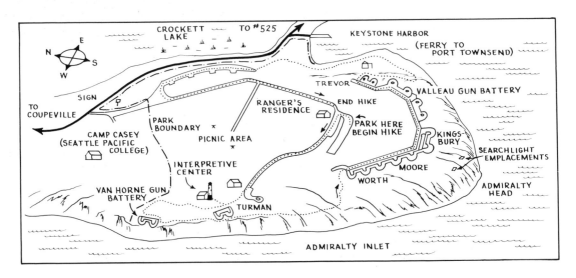

Old gun mounts at Fort Casey

it. Installed in the late 1890s, the fort was the key point in a coastal defense system designed to keep enemies from reaching Bremerton ,Navy Yard and surrounding "Big Four" cities.

Continue the hike on the bluff trail behind Battery Valleau, now a wide jeep track with massed borders of wild rose. It drops easily to shore in state park campgrounds. Walk left through the campground to the junction of the highway but instead of following the pavement turn left on a path that leads back uphill to the mortar installations first seen below the entrance

road to the fort. It passes in front of the bunkers, then joins that road to return to the parking area.

And after lunch, more than a mile of seashore below the fort is available for more steam-venting before returning to those four walls.

Round trip 2 miles
Allow 2 hours (more for museum)
Good all year
Paved road, dirt and gravel paths

57

Admiralty Inlet from Whidbey Island State Park

20 SOUTH WHIDBEY STATE PARK

In several summer visits, while Deception Pass State Park was crawling with human snails bearing homes on their backs, we found South Whidbey State Park going its dreamy way; the 100 acres and 42 campsites were occupied by the knowing, but seldom to overflowing. On a warm, beautiful Labor Day, the parking lot beside the "day-use" picnic area exhibited one car, and picnic tables were empty. This may not be typical, but the hiker will find virtually virgin territory — at least for awhile.

Take ferry from Mukilteo to Whidbey Island and drive north on State 525 to Freeland. Watch for park sign about .7 mile north of town and turn left on Bush Point Road. The latter joins Smuggler's Cove Road later, going north, and reaches the park entrance in about 5 miles. Turn into the entrance in front of ranger's residence, then right to parking area.

On the slope above the parking area are picnic tables. Begin the hike with the footpath to the left, winding along the edge of the steep cliff above the shore. Watch the young ones — there are no protective fences and a short slip is a long one, with the only landing a bed of mean devil's club spikes 100 feet below.

How long has it been since you heard the soughing of wind through tall trees? Or did it seem only a phrase coined by poets? Small cleared spots with picnic tables and fireplace grills have private views overlooking Admiralty Inlet. The sandy trail dips steeply, then curves back where the bluff recedes, and disappears in about ½ mile in salal and stinging nettle. (Unless the work of clearing and finishing the bluff trail has been completed. If so, continue to its end and return to the parking lot.)

The beach trail begins on the water side of the parking area and returns by way of the adjacent campground. Definitely a "posh" — not rugged — trail, but through beautiful woods. It drops swiftly to the beach in ½ mile, where big cedars, hemlocks, and firs, sword fern and salal, keep company with trilliums, ladyslipper, and twinflower. Chipmunks and squirrels, bluejays, woodpeckers, and flickers cock their heads at intruders, then go about their business. The trail ends on the beach at a bulkhead, and the narrow strip of beach on both sides invites the beachcomber with promises of driftwood and agates. Swimming and clamming are permitted. The water is shallow and the beach is agreeably sandier than most other Puget Sound beaches.

When ready to return, find the other trail behind another beach bulkhead about 1000 feet north of the first one. It leads up the steep hill through similar forest and comes back through the park's overnight camping area.

Round trip 1¾ miles
Allow 1½ hours
Good all year, best in spring
Dirt trails

Dogwood

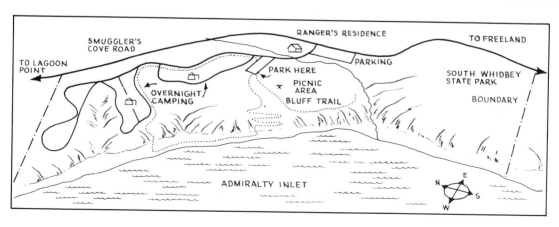

21 HOLMES HARBOR

Whidbey Island, viewed on the map or from the air, seems oddly twisted in shape. But by its contortions it has achieved a certain status: no point on this "second largest island in the country" is more than 3 miles from saltwater.

Islanders, however, don't tell the visitor their real secret. They know the newcomer, drawn by intriguing bits and pieces, becomes hopelessly enmeshed in a spider web of scenic beauty and history. And that, forsooth, is the secret. No island has the "feel" of history this one does.

There is nothing to designate Holmes Harbor or set it apart. The hiker is only searching for a good walk on the beach. Then Pow!

Time this trip for low tide. It is short, and the rest of the day can be spent farther up the Whidbey line. Take the Mukilteo ferry to the island or drive south from Anacortes. At Freeland exit, turn off highway, go into town to East Harbor Road. Drive toward the water, turning left on Stewart Road as it curves along the shore and reaches a wide gravel area with ample parking space between a hill to the left and the Freeland public boat launch. Park here and hike first to the right as far as a plank barrier, the public beach limit, about ¼ mile. Then head west between the water and the hill to the left. One of several cabins between boat ramp and hill was built by an early settler and still is occupied by descendants.

Make sure the tide is receding before walking west — the shore is only a thin strip against the hill. A quiet little bay lies on the other side. An old pier, at the foot of Woodard Avenue Road, about ¼ mile, juts into the water and must be climbed under or over to continue. (If water is up to the bluff, cross over the hill on the road leading from the boat launch as an alternate route. Good views can be had of the harbor from the top. The road drops down to the same pier.)

The pier, now occupied by sand-and-gravel-loading machinery, is "more than 60 years old," say old-timers. A socialist colony began in buildings near the dock in 1901. It ended in failure and squabbles. Continue from the dock around the curve of the bay to the large boat works, formerly a machine shop, at the far end. Unassuming locale, but replete with history. Before the machine shop was a store and a postoffice. A nearby resident, Mrs. Ethel Spencer, recalls that her husband's father, who came to Washington in 1884, became the first postmaster at Freeland. She and her husband followed in 1916, when he began the machine shop.

The mailboat **Rover** and before that, the **Alvarene** and the **Ruby** put into Holmes Harbor. There were woods all around and logging was the big industry until the 1920s. The Mexican ship **Providencia** later took on peeled logs for mining props and other lumber.

From the marine shop the west shoreline is private, lined with homes clear to its opening with Saratoga Passage, so return to the car for more island exploration.

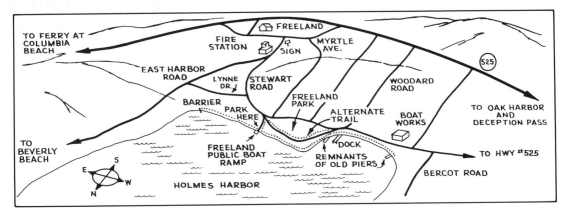

Holmes Harbor

Holmes Harbor was christened during the Wilkes Expedition in 1841 in honor of Silas Holmes, an assistant surgeon. Somehow the Indian name, so patently efficient, is more appealing: Ah-Lus-Dukh, "Go inside."

Round trip 1½ miles
Allow 1½ hours
Good all year
Sand and rock beach

22   SKAGIT CITY

Not all good walks are in woods or mountains. One of my favorites is in lush farm country, flat as a pancake, where once existed a flourishing town, the oldest settlement on the Skagit River. Now only the schoolhouse remains, for the ebb and flow of towns depend on flukes of nature. One town's pep pill may be another's poison: a log jam killed Skagit City and put Mount Vernon on the map.

Drive Interstate 5 to 6 miles south of Mt. Vernon and take Conway exit west. The overpass splits immediately off the freeway. Bear right to the bridge spanning the South Fork of Skagit River. Turn right at its end, in front of a quaint church with tall spire, and follow Skagit City road. You now are on Fir Island.

The 10-foot-high dike to the right is your protector against the muddy, swirling river. Left are rich, green fields of peas, cabbage, corn, grazing cattle and horses, and ducks waddling in ponds. Along the way are farmhouses, some clean and neat, some run-down, some old-style with squared roofs. And always the meadowlarks, singing.

At 2.2 miles, turn left on Moore Road and continue .3 mile to the schoolhouse, now deserted (closed in 1940) but maintained by the Skagit City School Pioneer Association. The bell remains that once tolled for classes. Moss has fingered its way under the roof shingles, but clematis and roses still bloom, and old trees still give shade.

Park on road or school driveway and begin the walk by retracing Moore Road to Skagit Road. Turn left, keep the dike on your right, and walk north past more farmhouses and a public fishing dock sign on the right, to where the road turns sharply left, about 1.2 miles. Before continuing, climb the dike. The river spreads before you. Left, the powerful Skagit pours down from the north and divides abruptly into the North and South Forks, creating Fir Island.

Do you see only water, and muddy, weeded shore? A tangled green jungle across the river? Look again, into the past. Here, in 1869, the trading post known as Barker's sprang up to serve pioneer homesteaders. Then came a telegraph office and a postal station. By 1879 Skagit City was an important town, with hotels, stores, restaurant, saloons, churches, warehouse, and wharf. Steamers, sternwheelers, ferries, and a snag boat plied the river. Skagit City looked to the future with confidence. Mt. Vernon was only a name and a few houses. Then the log jam came apart.

Settlers, investigating the rich delta land of Fir Island, knew of the big log jam. As early as 1856, men hunting gold had gone up river and camped where the river was blocked. So pioneers

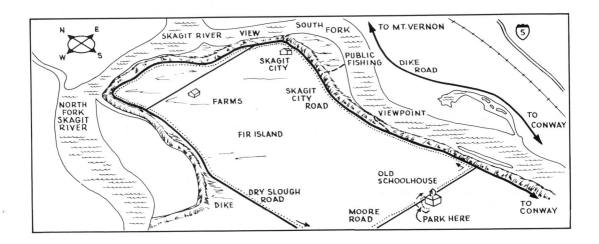

Skagit River and Mount Baker

homesteaded south of the log jam. All navigation stopped short at the obstruction and turned around at the point where Skagit City bloomed.

In 1874, five pioneers under contract began the task of removing the log jam. They worked almost 5 years. The two men responsible for the contract and payment for labor drowned, and the others were never paid. Nevertheless, it was a great day in 1879 when steamers finally could go up the Skagit to Marblemount, take-off for the "gold fields." The coming of the railroad in 1888 also brought traffic to Mount Vernon, and Skagit City languished.

Finish the walk — visions of a vanished town lingering — by following the road, which parallels the river ½ mile, then turns sharp left again, past acres of peas, strawberry fields, and charming cottage farmhouses. In the distance is snowy Mt. Baker, rising above Cascade foothills. Reach Moore Road again in slightly more than a mile. Turn left to the schoolhouse, ½ mile.

Round trip 3.4 miles
Allow 2 hours
Good all year
Paved road

Skagit Flats and Olympic Mountains from Observation Park on Little Mountain

23   LITTLE MOUNTAIN

The glaciers that slid down from the north thousands of years ago left, as a legacy, many natural viewpoints. On this mountain, a few miles out of Mount Vernon, are excellent examples of glacial filing action. Alas, contemporary man, once the outdoor lover, seems maliciously intent on his new role as "outdoor smotherer," and covers it up with broken bottle fragments and garbage.

Follow directions for Devil's Mountain (Trip 24) to Little Mountain Road where it leaves Blackburn Road. Watch closely for a well-used gravel road on the right, about .8 mile, which forms a gentle Y with the main paved road, and follow it uphill to a gate about .1 mile farther. If the gate is locked, park off the road here and hike. If open, continue to a large U-turn .4 mile and park on a wide spot at its upper end. A few steps into the woods to the left of the U-turn, find an unmarked trail, running parallel with the road. The trail climbs steeply through beautiful, open forest ½ mile to the lookout tower on top.

The easy way, of course, is to drive all the way to the top and hike the trail down instead. A non-hiker in the party can meet the others at the U-turn on the road. But hiking down, watch carefully to the left for the road at the U-turn. Though only a few feet away through the trees, it is not marked and the hiker can easily miss it, as this hoofer discovered. (A small heap of stones placed after my error may still be there to mark the exit.)

Some sleuthing is needed also to find the trail at the top, since false trails mislead; simply bear farthest to the right past the microwave relay station behind the tower. A few slippery steep places at first are left behind as one follows the edge of a bluff with views of Darrington peaks, then the way drops down into forest.

Second-growth trees have caught up with the observation tower and hide views of Mount Baker. But to the west, Mount Vernon and its surrounding neat farms are spread below, with wide views of Skagit Flats, Fir Island to the south, Fidalgo and Whidbey Islands in the Sound beyond, and Olympic Mountains outlining the horizon. The lookout tower is made to order for nervous folk: the stairway is enclosed until one reaches viewing perches at the top.

Massive, flat rock outcrops around the parking area near the tower seem like paving blocks. Look closely, even if it means scraping away broken beer bottles! Deep, straight scratches in the rock surface, all in one direction, indicate that once a glacier was here.

Round trip 1 mile

Allow 1½ hours

High point 934 feet

Elevation gain 500 feet

Best March to November — often good in winter

Dirt trail

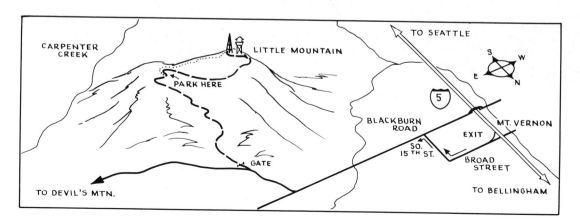

24 DEVIL'S MOUNTAIN

How did Devil's Mountain earn its name? Was some settler miserable or angry from a bad experience, or simply in a bad mood? Many names on our maps may have derived from such ignoble beginnings, when pioneers, spreading their ripples wider in virgin territory, clapped names thoughtlessly or in haste on physical features as yet unnamed.

But if you don't like the names on the map, coin your own. That's part of the fun. Years hence, one may giggle:

"Remember on 'Snow Goose Mountain' when we surprised that porcupine in the middle of the road and had to hang on to our pooch?"

The thousands of elegant snow geese we had just seen feeding on the vast, mud-and-reed shallows of Skagit Flats, almost at the foot of the mountain, inspired OUR substitute for the devil that haunted the pioneer name-dropper. We felt only such a bird could enjoy the matchless views of saltwater, lowlands, and white peaks.

Drive north on Interstate 5 and exit at sign for Mount Vernon. Avoid left turn at underpass for town and turn right, uphill, on Broad Street, then right on South 15th Street and continue to

T intersection. Turn left on Blackburn Road and in 1 mile turn right on Little Mountain Road, following white center line. Continue 3 miles to a T intersection. Turn right on Amick Road. Follow the winding, gravel road ½ mile, ignoring side roads, to a gravel road on the left, marked by faded, white posts. The sign, "Devil's Mountain Truck Trail," may be gone.

Park on shoulder here where there is ample room and begin walking. (Do not block the service road, which is used constantly). The climb is gradual, through second-growth forest and close-grown brush 2 miles to a gate. The final ½ mile from the gate to lookout point is quite steep, but a hiker can appreciate the wind in the firs, the waist-high sword ferns dipping fronds in salute, and glimpses through trees of the vistas to come.

At the top, the former lookout tower has been replaced by a relay station, and while the bald knoll makes a pleasant picnic spot, the glorious "Snow Goose" aerial scenography once enjoyed by climbing the tower steps is almost hidden by tree growth since this book's first writing. However, in glimpses through the circle of greenery Mount Rainier may be seen in views to the south, range on range of snowy crests east and north to Canada, and west over Skagit Flats to the Olympics. Nearby Mount Baker dominates all.

A pleasant side hike can be made to tiny Lake Ten. Find the trail beginning at the Smokey Bear sign about 100 feet after passing the gate on the final ascent to the lookout. The trail drops steeply 1/3 mile to the 16-acre lake.

For better views, the hiker may prefer another 5-mile route to an eastern peak. Take the left fork less than ½ mile from parking spot on Amick Road. The road climbs steadily 1½ miles through woods, drops a bit then climbs steeply again to a recent clear cut with view of Big Lake, Mount Baker and Mount Whitehorse.

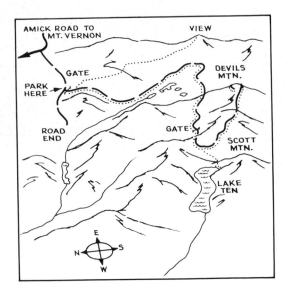

Round trip 5 miles
Allow 3-4 hours
High point 1727 feet
Elevation gain 1000 feet
Best March to November; often good in winter
Gravel road

View from Devil's Mountain — White Chuck Mountain, center, Glacier Peak, and Whitehorse Mountain

Mount Baker and snow geese at the Skagit Game Range

25   SKAGIT GAME RANGE

He who claims himself a Puget Sounder has no right to the title until he has seen and heard the snow geese fly—a spectacle as stirring as any in nature—a sound so awesome it raises prickles from neck to tailbone.

All winter they can be seen riding the waves of Skagit Bay, drifting in with the tide to feed on roots and fresh grass shoots on the marshy shore. They congregate in great masses, coming in on flights of 5 to 50 birds, but when they take off do so by the thousands. From January 15 (end of hunting season) until they leave in April (latest departure date recorded was May 5) is the best viewing time. They breed on Wrangell Island, off north Siberia, leave there in late August, stop in Alaska and British Columbia before arriving on the Skagit. When they decide to leave, they do so en masse, within a 24-hour period. A lucky sight!

Drive to Conway, a few miles south of Mount Vernon (exit west from Interstate 5 on State 530). Cross South Fork of Skagit River and continue west 1½ miles on Fir Island Road to Mann Road (Game Department and Skagit Grange signs). Park by ranger headquarters at end of road, about ½ mile, on edge of Wiley Slough.

For one of two hikes leading to prime viewing areas, walk past headquarters across Wiley Slough to the dike and continue on road to the left. The dike road on the right, barred with a locked chain, is the return end of this horseshoe-shaped loop hike. Note wood duck nests along the slough channel—small boxes above water, to which ducks return every year to raise their broods. At a second dike is a boat launch and parking lot (if preferred, drive this far). Begin a 2-mile loop hike behind a gate on top of the dike to the right. At ¾ mile it turns right, paralleling the marshy shore, to a junction at sluice gates. (A footpath, left of sluice gate, continues ¼ mile farther out to the shore—a good side-trip.) From this junction, the dike leads back to headquarters.

Rare indeed are such experiences as this hike offers. One almost skates above the marsh, staying well inside Fresh Water Slough, with smaller Teal Slough on the right. A solitary, great blue heron rises ponderously from tall rushes, flaps away, then wheels back. Black and white bufflehead ducks, widgeons, greater scaup ducks, marsh hawks, scoters, eiders, killdeer are everywhere, paddling, waddling, or flying. Silvery pyramids of dunlins rise, wheel on the instant and jet right or left, then pyramid again. A buff-colored, short-eared owl glides above the dikes on silent wings. With luck a snowy owl, infrequent visitor from the Arctic, may be seen, turning his head almost in a complete circle as he watches for game. Sometimes a bald eagle, identified by white head and tail, soars by hoping for a crippled goose.

For the second hike, return to Conway. Drive south toward Stanwood on State 530 about 5 miles past Milltown, cross railroad tracks and leave the highway which turns left. Continue straight on a rough dirt road ½ mile to the Game Department's "Big Ditch Hunting Access Area." Park here and hike along the dike that parallels the marshy shore. Binoculars are a must, both for the myriads of redwinged blackbirds and marsh wrens perched on cattails and rushes stretching far into Skagit Bay, and for the thousands of snow geese on tide flats. Hike also to the left of the dam above the parking area. A narrow path between a slough and trees takes one beyond reeds to a cleared point of land. To the right, on saltmarsh across from the South Jetty, is a magnificent pageant — a wall-to-wall, rippling carpet of snow geese, framed by the backdrop of equally snowy Mount Baker.

When the geese rise, the din first sounds oddly like the yapping of dogs, then swells to a thundering ovation. Long after leaving, the ears ring with the sound nothing else can duplicate.

Round trip: Hike 1—2 miles; Hike 2—2½ miles
Allow 2 hours each
Good October 1 to April 30; best after hunting
    season ends, January 15
Dike road; may be wet

Snow geese at the Skagit Game Range

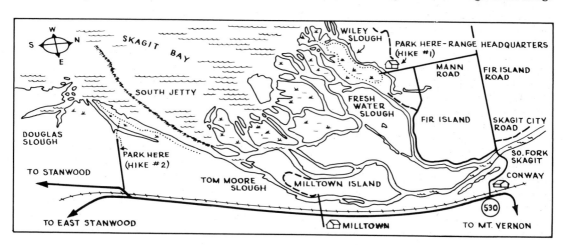

26 CAMANO ISLAND STATE PARK

Camano Island, 27 miles long, lies coddled in an almost completely landlocked salt lagoon, close to the mainland on the east and protected from pounding seas north and west by more rugged Fidalgo and Whidbey Islands. Winter as well as summer there is a gentle amenity about Camano, located as it is in the Olympic rain-shadow.

Drive Interstate 5 about 14 miles north of Marysville exit to exit marked "Stanwood-Camano Island" and turn west on State 532 through Stanwood. Cross the slough on General Mark Clark Bridge (he has a home on the island) and continue 4½ miles to a junction, "Terry's Corner," marked by a huge and helpful island directory. (The interesting pioneer cemetery is to the right of the signboard.) Drive south 8 miles from the junction to Elger Bay and turn right (west) 2 miles to Camano Island State Park. The entrance road descends sharply to the North Beach area, where grass and madronas and picnic tables flank the beach. Park here and walk back up the road to a sharp bend and a sign marking the beginning of Point Lowell Trail.

The salal-bordered path skirts the top of the bluff under large firs and hemlocks, now hanging above clefts padded with devil's club and mossy greens fringing cool springs trickling to the rocky shore, and now plunging into a forest of giant trees. Spectacular views over Whidbey Island to the Strait of Juan de Fuca.

In about ¼ mile a bridge crosses the gully of an old log chute which dates back to 1910. In another ¼ mile is a fork. Turn right, descending a series of rustic log steps to the driftwood, grass, and rocks of the wide beach on Point Lowell.

To return, one has a choice. At low tide, hike the beach. But be careful on an incoming tide— at high tide there **isn't** any beach!

For the alternate return, walk the paved road from Point Lowell about ¾ mile to a sign marking a Nature Trail. (This ¼-mile path offers a pleasant, 20-minute diversion among trees individually marked to show how forests looked 150 years ago. The horseshoe-shaped route brings the hiker back to the road.) Continue north ¼ mile to where a powerline road intersects the paved one. Turn right on it for variety, if desired, or continue the paved road. Both come out at the camping area by the ranger's residence. From there, follow the paved road to the parking lot.

Islanders can be justly proud of their personal state park, which 500 residents roughed out in a series of work parties. Future plans include a "boundary trail" providing a 6-mile hike through forests around the entire 200-acre park border.

Round trip 1½ miles; alternate route 2¼ miles
Allow 2 hours; for alternate, 2½ hours
Good all year
Road, trail, rocky beach

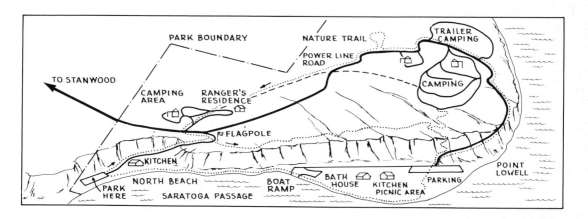

Saratoga Passage from Camano Island State Park

27   BOULDER RIVER FALLS

A high waterfall, a great river, a tall tree. All part of Nature's majesty.

But don't overlook her creations in miniature. The Boulder River hike is memorable not alone for its pockets of yet-unravaged forest, its dazzling waterfall and voluptuous pools, but a Lilliputian fairyland as well. Plan a day for this, for this hike is like an expansion bracelet—the first-timer returns often to explore more links.

Such has been the pace of logging in recent years, the Boulder River valley is now unique —holding the last low-elevation virgin forest close to Puget Sound. For that reason it is proposed for inclusion in a Whitehorse Wilderness Area.

From Arlington, drive east on State 530. About 2 miles east of Hazel, turn south at sign for French Creek Campground, 1 mile. Continue beyond campground on one-lane, somewhat rocky road which climbs slightly above the creek, passing some dirt branch tracks and in about 2½ miles reaching a fork. The Boulder River trail begins on right branch. Drive down it a short distance to park.

The trail (probably an old railroad) starts soggily, following a gorge through young forest studded with 10- to 15-foot stumps still showing ax marks of early logging methods where springboards were wedged. The old roadbed narrows to a foot trail as it hugs a high bank 'round a hill. The green verdure that blankets the bank, rocks, and tree trunks is a world of exquisite delicacy.

Under protective arms of pipsissewa and ferns is an outdoor tapestry — a forest in miniature, waiting for a modern explorer armed with magnifying glass — surprising varieties of mosses and lichens side by side; each as different and intricate as snowflakes, from smooth, glossy leaves to feathery ostrich boas, in a gamut of greens — silvery gray, yellow, blue, emerald.

At ½ mile a boulder marks a right spur which descends to the river in ¼ mile. The main trail continues left, climbing gradually higher above the river, past 6-foot stumps and a mycologist's paradise (in season) of saucer-sized mushrooms in beige, blue-gray, orange, oyster-white. The curtain of green opens to a view high above rapids — and Boulder Falls. Down to the river now, and into an enchanted valley. A leanto shelter nestled at the edge of enticing pools swirling around huge boulders; the root mass of a fallen forest giant rearing 15 feet above the river shore; and 100 yards beyond the shelter, the falls.

No wispy trickle this, but a Gemini: two plumes outlining an hourglass spilling 80 feet down a rocky cliff. The trail continues far beyond the falls, past more shelters.

Just to the falls is a taste of honey. One sip leads to more.

Round trip 2½ miles
Allow 2 hours
High point 1425 feet
Elevation gain 100 feet
Best March to October, often open in winter

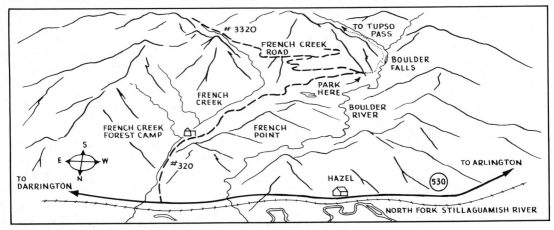

Waterfalls on a tributary of Boulder Creek

Queencup beadlily

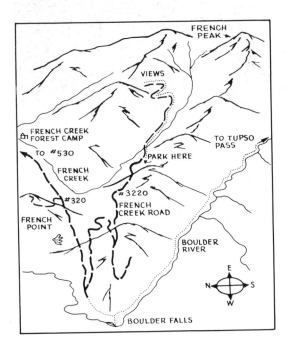

28   FRENCH CREEK RIDGE

If variety be the spice of life, French Creek Ridge offers that seasoning to the Boulder Falls hike. Though both begin from the same point they are as different in hiking character and scenery as night from day. This one is a steady climb with rewarding views, while the trail to the falls is nearly level, through deep woods.

Drive east on State 530 from Arlington and turn south on Forest Service road No. 320 about 2 miles east of Hazel. Continue past French Creek Campground about 2½ miles to a fork with the Boulder River trail. Take the left, road No. 3220. The gravel road starts climbing steeply through woods, mounting ever higher as it doubles back and forth on hairpin turns. The narrow road is a bit rough in spots and there are no safety guards between the road and the sheer cliff, but is negotiable with care and the views grow ever more superb.

Across the wide valley on the north, Mt. Higgins seems close enough to touch. In fall, the crevices and folds of its tilted rock strata are tinged red with autumn-colored foliage, looking as though the mountain is scratched and bleeding. Going up, the green, almost perfect cone of French Peak does a "strip-tease" as she is revealed in stages. Leering at her from behind are the snowy cusps of Mt. Whitehorse. The road skirts along the north side of Boulder Ridge and enters a draw. At the head of the defile, about 6 miles, French Creek, an icy infant, plunges down the mountainside. Park here where there is space off the road and begin the hike. The road continues its steep climb across the bridge, past clearcut forest area logged in 1961 and replanted the next year, and in ½ mile enters forested area again.

The graveled but steadily rockier and rougher road continues a little over 2 miles more to its ending at a jumbled mass of gray, weather-beaten slash. Trudge the steep final 1/3 mile to road's end to enjoy the view. The intriguing glacier of Whitehorse to the east is clearly seen, even its crevasses; the sharp crest of the ridge behind the glacier marches south to meet headlong with high, sharp peaks of Three Fingers.

The way back to the car is not so strained,

Mount Higgins from French Creek road

and no one can take away those views implanted in your memory bank. There may even be an extra cherry on the sundae driving back down through lower forest—a doe and her fawn ambling ahead on the road. Stop the motor and approach on foot, quietly, a step at a time. Mama deer will accept the get-acquainted invitation and come to meet you halfway, as ours did.

French Creek got its name, according to a pioneer of 1865, from the fact that three of its first settlers were French Canadians. Very unimaginative. For its views, at least, they should have named it Voila!

Round trip 4 miles
Allow 4 hours
High point 3600 feet
Elevation gain 1000 feet
Good June to October, often later
Dry gravel road, rocky in places

75

29   MONTE CRISTO RAILWAY

The crumbled remains of the old mining town of Monte Cristo draw visitors like a magnet, and each summer hikers by the thousands climb to eagle-eyrie mines in surrounding peaks.

Yet the town's lifeline, the Everett and Monte Cristo Railway, built in 1893, is all but forgotten. Here and there along the highway one glimpses remnants of ties, rails, and trestles. Earlier editions of this book led readers to two long-neglected railroad tunnels high above the Stillaguamish River. But the route lies through private property, and permission by owners who previously did not mind using their road as access, has been withdrawn due to lack of courtesy and possibility of damage and injury. A lesson to outdoor lovers: Will they learn in time, or will many similar areas eventually be sealed off?

Following the route of the railroad can be an intriguing quest, like pursuing a will-o-the-wisp. Best bet is to find an old-timer who "knew it when." From the tunnels ending at the old town of Robe on the north side of the South Fork of the Stillaguamish River, old maps and schedules indicate the railroad crossed the river and went east on the south side. This hike is on a road old-timers point to as part of this south-side railroad bed, and though all signs of it have vanished, a beautiful stroll remains, decorated by waterfalls.

From Granite Falls, drive east on the Mountain Loop Highway. Pass the Verlot Ranger Station about 12 miles, and just over a mile beyond, cross a river bridge. A sign here marks a right turn for Pilchuck Mountain Road. Park in the wide area by an old tavern opposite the road and begin hike on Pilchuck Road across the highway, but turn right off that road almost immediately, on a narrow, branch road doubling back on the south side of the river.

In less than half a mile the road widens into a graveled apron. A cascade pours over rocky boulders and under the road. (For a shorter hike, drive to this point where parking space is ample.) Follow the road beside the turbulent river. It ascends a few feet to where remains of an old wooden bridge can be discerned, then levels in a straight stretch.

Beyond, the road tunnels through woods,

banked by a lush wall of greenery that drinks thirstily from fountains gushing here and there from nature's faucets. In dry season, the faucets are all but drained. But the wetter the weather, the more enjoyable the walk, along a series from trickles to rivulets to dancing, splashing plunges. In just under 2 miles, a log barrier blocks vehicles, but not hikers. The old railbed disappears under grass. The best waterfall of all lies only 1/8 mile ahead—a roaring, tumbling torrent over Hawthorne Creek, which long ago angrily tore out all traces of man's puny wooden bridge.

Round trip 4 miles
Allow 2 hours
Good all year except heavy rain or snow
Road wet and muddy in spots

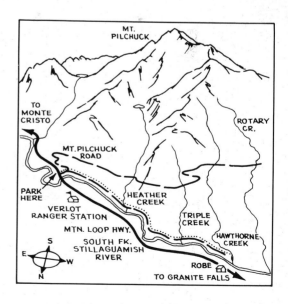

Lush growth on Verlot Road.

*Good view - short climb - route is not pretty
Trashy.*

30   HIGH ROCK

It's easy to see why Indians revered High Rock as a medicine rock, as local legends say. The hill stands haughtily alone, dominating the wide valley south of Monroe. But modern folk climb it often with their youngsters, finding the "medicine man" likes families. This pleasant walk leads by road and trail up an easy grade to a spacious, bald top with plenty of room to move around for views.

Drive south from Monroe on State 203 across bridge spanning the Skykomish River. Slow down when the first road to the right is sighted at .8 mile (sign "Swiss Hall"). Just beyond turn into a gravel road on the left leading past old farm buildings. The driveway passes

Mount Baker and farms near Monroe from High Rock

the edge of a large, rush-filled pond on the right, then goes up a rise over railroad tracks. Park here, well away in the corner of a sharp curve, and hike where the road climbs left, uphill, paralleling the railroad. Just back of the rushes and brush at the parking corner is a fine, cool spring; fill canteens for the picnic lunch on the summit.

The road is shaded by alder, maple, dogwood, and salmonberries hanging over daisies. At ½ mile is a fork. Take the left branch under cool cottonwoods and alders; smiling buttercups replace the daisies. At .1 mile more is another fork. Behind the road barricade on the left, the private road ends at a quarry in a few feet. Go right, uphill instead, on the gravel road. In .3 mile from the fork where the road swings right, a wide path goes left past a house at the bend and ascends gently through woods, following a fence, then turns right to climb more steeply. In less than ¼ mile, at an open area with stumps, turn left off the wide track on a trail through deeper woods. In another ¼ mile it emerges suddenly from woods at a high rock-and-shale shelf — the only ticklish part of the hike. A few carefully-placed steps (stout shoes with firm-grip soles are the answer) are needed to get up the 10-foot wall.

On top is a breeze-swept plateau of fully an acre or more, carpeted with daisies, kinnikinnick, Oregon grape, salal, and ferns, with here and there little grassy hollows ideal for picnicking. Views are comfortable, pleasant: an expansive green valley cuddling Monroe immediately north and Sultan farther east; the Skykomish River wending west to merge with the Snoqualmie; the bulky mass of Mt. Pilchuck rising above farms north of Monroe; and if the air be clear, Mt. Baker's gleaming peak.

The road and property traversed on the hike are privately owned. Access is granted by courtesy of the owner — PROVIDED the courtesy is returned by good outdoor manners. Show appreciation by taking along a plastic bag, filling it with trash left lying about and carrying it out. If enough good citizens do this, they will offset the bad manners of the "selfish ones," who may, if their numbers grow, cause the owner to rescind his kind permission.

The owner assumes no responsibility for accident or injury occuring to individuals on his property.

Round trip 2.7 miles
Allow 2½ hours
High point 681 feet
Elevation gain 601 feet
Good all year except when too snowy
Gravel road and dirt trail

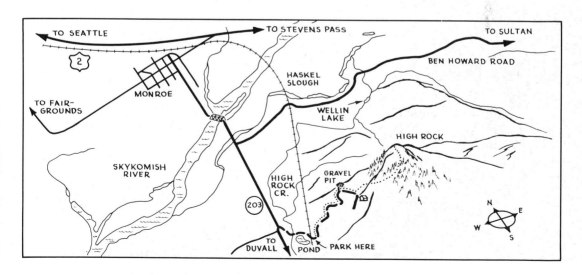

31   YOUNGS CREEK

We talk of nature in glib terms, sometimes. How mountains grow or wear down; how rivers cut deep to carve canyons. In one's lifetime, it is rare to see noticeable change in natural fea-tures. In certain places, however, Nature helps with "action shots." This backwoods road hike allows one to see the old gal "doing her thing" — carving a gorge. Take a picnic lunch. The hike ends at a lovely, little-used campground. Water is available.

The route is the same as for Haystack Mountain: Drive US 2 to Sultan, cross Skykomish

Forest along Youngs Creek road

River bridge in town and turn right (west) on Ben Howard Road. Go past Haystack Mountain Road and at 2½ miles (from Sultan) turn left on Cedar Ponds Lake Road (small sign SLH-1000). In about a mile, find space to park shortly after a sharp right turn through a tunnel of trees. Begin the walk on the winding road, bearing right at a fork within ½ mile.

The graveled road saunters through a lush, open area, fringed by a low range of fir-clad hills in the distance. Through the wide valley Youngs Creek meanders. Ferns and wildflowers edge the road, arched over by lacy cedars, alders, and maple. Some trees are only bare skeletons, dripping with moss, like botanical octo-puses clothed in a forest of seaweed. In times past, a mine was worked far above the road.

In just under 2 miles is a sturdy bridge over Youngs Creek. Stop for long looks. Here is geology in action, capsuled for the viewer. On the east side of the bridge the icy water flows through a thick tangle of firs in a contented sort of surge, swirls gaily in a wide curve under the bridge, then, as though surprised, gathers in a chattering fright before dropping down a rocky shelf into a deep rock chasm and roaring down the gorge.

At the south end of the bridge, on the right, can be seen a faint trail leading up the bank and behind a big tree. Fishermen and old-time loggers report the gorge is even more spectacular beyond the bridge. This path gets there, but the going is extremely risky. A fall here could easily end in a tumble down the gorge. Even passing through is risky — there is poison oak. One extra caution: do not allow children to clamber around the jumble of fallen logs near the bridge. The logs are very slippery and dangerous.

When the ears are surfeited with the sounds of rushing waters, continue along the road ½ mile to a second bridge crossing. The gorge is not as deep here but the river's rocky rapids are pictur-esque. Youngs Creek Campground is an inviting, cool area nearby, with picnic tables among big trees on the slope above the bridge, and the music of Nature for background. In the time it takes to lunch, she makes no measurable dent in the face of the earth.

Come back a million years from now!

Round trip 5 miles
Allow 3 hours
High point 550 feet
Elevation gain 184 feet
Good all year
Gravel and dirt road

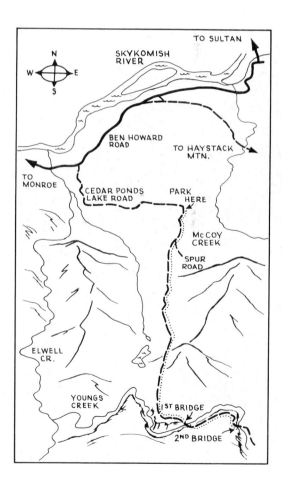

Skykomish River and town of Gold Bar, on right, from Haystack Mountain

32   HAYSTACK LOOKOUT

Ever play in a haystack as a child? Remember the endless pleasure, the surprises? Climb topside or burrow into the mound anywhere; you came out on something new every time.

Haystack Mountain (once called Cougar until some mapmaker evidently familiar with haystack delights renamed it) is like that. Climb or burrow this mound of "hay" and pop out on many surprises. Unfortunately, roads on south and west are restricted from entry between July and October, but the north approach yields the most surprises anyway. Pack a lunch and allow a full day to enjoy them.

Drive US 2 to Sultan and cross Skykomish River on bridge in town. At junction with Ben Howard Road, turn right (west). The pavement jogs past farms, then crosses McCoy Creek on a small bridge. At 1.6 miles from Sultan, turn left on first road after McCoy Creek. The narrow gravel road angles uphill to a plank creek bridge at .7 mile.

Now the "haystack surprises" begin. Ignore a spur to the right about 1½ miles from highway; .3 miles farther is another spur to the left, the route of an old railway grade. (For separate hike, see "Haystack Logging Road" following this.)

The main road ascends gradually, curving left. Chuckholes increase, but the vaulted dome of cedar and alder, spotlighted by huge yellow skunk cabbage in damp recesses, seals off mundane cares. At 2.3 miles, trees give way suddenly to high reeds under open sky. Surprise! A lake lies almost unseen behind them. Park and walk the planks laid end to end beyond and behind the reeds for a look at Mud Lake (also called Lost Lake).

The road climbs steeply, levels off, then abruptly comes up to kiss the radiator, it seems, forcing low-gear, watchful driving as it comes out of deep woods on loose rocks. Then "into the haystack" — a weird but intriguing sensation of crawling around inside high walls of a box canyon. The plant ecosystem, looking into the draw, seems dry and totally separated.

At 5.7 miles, where briefly level, is a large culvert. The road ascends again and in another mile, at the top of a short, very steep incline, doubles back left in a hairpin turn. An old graveled service road splits off, continuing in the direction of the incline. Park at this Y where roomy and almost level and begin hike. The track is rough and steep and impassable farther for passenger cars. Carry lunch and water. Keep left at second and third forks (from the last it is straight up and gutted). The fourth and last fork, atop the ridge, ½ mile farther, is marked by a tiny lake. Turn right for the lookout.

Open views enchant and tarry the hiker from the parking site to the abandoned tower. Sultan and Monroe squat by Skykomish River far below; lakes spatter the landscape as far as Puget Sound, and peaks jab the sky from Mount Rainier to Mount Baker, with Mount Stickney seemingly close enough to touch.

Round trip 5 miles
Allow 4 hours
High point 3590 feet
Elevation gain 1990 feet
Best April to October
Dirt and gravel road

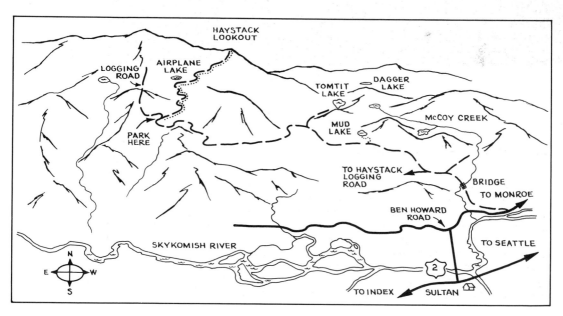

33 HAYSTACK LOGGING ROAD

An old logging railroad right-of-way used within the memory of today's retired loggers wanders in the "pleasant zone" along the base of Haystack Mountain, through splendid mossy forest.

Follow directions for Haystack Lookout from Sultan. Swing uphill on Haystack Lookout Road, cross the plank bridge and continue main road 1.8 miles to the first spur which leaves main road on the left. Park off the road here and begin hike.

The single-track, dirt lane usually has mud puddles, and through winter and spring usually is flooded. So reserve this hike to do only after a long, dry spell. Wear waterproof boots and do not attempt to drive. The old road bores into stands of alder and vigorous young firs striving here and there to emulate yesteryear's giants, seen in huge, moss-mantled stumps. Vine maple, as tall and thick as it ever grows, rampages 30 feet high above the underbrush of sword fern that reaches almost overhead, and great mushrooms hide in crevices on the damp forest floor.

In 1½ miles is a triple fork. The oldtime railroad bed branched to various logging sites. The left and middle forks dead-end in little more than a mile, the left near the Skykomish River. The right branch splits again in ½ mile, each branch dead-ending in a mile.

Views are not of impressive peaks as from higher up. One is, instead, enveloped and almost blotted up into the forest — what better way to feel one with Nature!

A fisherman tells of wandering off the trail near here. He parted a thick tangle of bushes and stared straight into the eyes of a bear. Fortunately the bear was as startled as he, and shot from the thicket out of his sight.

Trillium

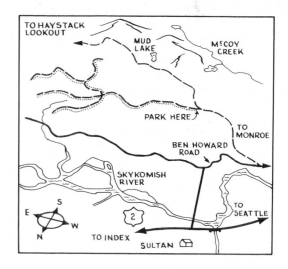

Round trip 3 miles to triple fork; add 2 miles each branch
Allow 2½ hours
High point 500 feet
Elevation gain 150 feet
Best late summer and fall
Usually muddy

Old railroad grade on Haystack Mountain

34 WINTERS LAKE TO KELLOGG LAKE

"You don't realize what you have here," said a New Yorker. "Drive in the countryside anywhere else and what do you see? Fences. It's like going through an endless, sealed corridor. But here? Only a few miles from town you can stop the car, walk a few feet off the road and in two minutes be lost in deep forest. Where but in the Northwest can that happen?"

Hike from Winters Lake to Kellogg Lake and our New Yorker's remarks take on significance. No fences. Step off the highway and disappear, like a wood sprite. It's something we've taken for granted. We're lucky. (But for how long?)

Drive east on US 2. About ½ mile east of Sultan, turn left on paved road at top of hill. (Sign "Sultan Basin Recreation-Sports Area.") In 2½ miles, Winters Lake is sighted behind heavy timber. Soon after sighting, about ½ mile is a branch road, right, for Kellogg Lake, but a second junction a few yards ahead forms a triangle with better parking space.

Before heading for Kellogg Lake, walk north a short distance on the road fringing Winters Lake. This small, 11-acre lake, named for an early

settler, has a character almost opposite that of Kellogg, at the other end of the hike. Mysterious, dark, and gloomy with its thick hem of firs, it could furnish a setting for a Wagnerian opera.

Now hike east from the triangle on Kellogg Lake road. On weekdays, it is almost a solo journey, as one cleaves a wake through timber. Big cedars, hemlocks, and stumps of once-grander monarchs are an imposing, silent accompaniment to one's soliloquy. In ½ mile, a narrow dirt lane appears on the left of the blacktop, marked by two enormous stumps, their charred sides softened by graceful swordfern. A large "Keep Washington Clean" sign once identified this road, along with the usual collection of cans, containers, and lunch wrappings of idiots who can't read or think. Follow the lane into the woods — the litter diminishes as it penetrates through overgrown berry bushes. Keep bearing right as the track bends in a horseshoe curve past a couple of spurs, then straightens out in ¼ mile, to end suddenly in a thick grove of cottonwoods at the edge of Kellogg Lake.

Kellogg, slightly larger (20 acres) than Winters, has an open, inviting disposition, albeit surrounded by marshy shores, sunken logs, and reeds. The lake is in two segments, connected by 1700 feet of narrow waterway, but fishermen may be seen anywhere on its shallow, 15-foot-deep waters. Several launch areas are available here and from the highway.

Return to the highway and walk another ¼ mile east for more views of the lake and surrounding mountains before returning to the car. On the way back, stop and listen often. Birds, squirrels, and chipmunks dart through the woods on either side. Their chirps and twitters seem to echo our New Yorker's remarks:

"Where else, indeed?"

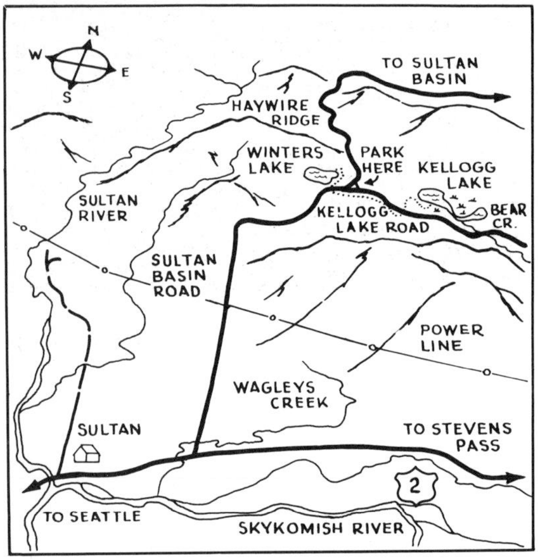

Round trip 2 miles
Allow 2 hours
High point 800 feet
Good all year
Level, paved road and dirt lane

Kellogg Lake

35   WALLACE FALLS

Exploring an area like Wallace Falls yields extra dividends in vignettes of local history. But only for the observant and inquisitive mind.

Hard to believe, trekking through moccasin-soft stillness of the woods, the life and times that once throbbed here. The Northwest "jungle" consumes and buries the past rapidly. One can pass its signs totally unseeing.

The falls, part of a future state park (land purchased but undeveloped), are visible in the green wall north of the highway approaching Goldbar from the west, seemingly unattainable. Yet the hike is an easy stroll three-fourths of the way. Only the last bit separates the men from boys—and women from blabber-mouths (like yours truly).

Drive east on US 2 to edge of Goldbar. Turn left at first intersection (Standard Station) and follow Wallace Lake signs through right turn and Y fork (go left) 1.2 miles to Episcopal Camp Huston sign where paved road turns sharp right. Park on wide shoulder left of sign. A dirt road goes left uphill for the lake and a graveled road ahead is gated. Begin hike ascending road behind gate. In ¼ mile, where it turns right to houses, go straight on an old logging road through woods, and across a powerline clearing ¼ mile more. It begins again with a fork. Go left. Gradually the road ascends, switchbacks right, and reaches a wide clearing in another mile. The clearing is an old railroad landing and junction with spur road connecting with Wallace Lake road, and supports of an old trestle still are seen.

Keep straight past the clearing. In 1 mile is another clearing. Turn sharp right off roadbed on a footpath that drops steeply from root clumps to flat-top boulders by noisy North Fork of the Wallace River — so pleasant a lunchsite many end the hike here. For human goats and waterfall fans, the trail across the rustic bridge climbs steeply but easily 500 steps, then hits a rocky slope with few handholds. Slowly, carefully does it. Above, the trail levels in open forest, then climbs again. Only 100 feet more to a tiny viewpoint by a big stump, with just a wire separating viewer from precipice. The cataract seems as high as Snoqualmie Falls, but is broken, dropping to various levels. Venture no farther. Loose rock and hidden soft slopes add danger.

Old-timers full of memories worked for the Gold Bar Logging Company and Wallace Falls Timber Company in the area north of Wallace River beginning 1916. The old trestle was built in 1921, says one old-timer. The railroad ran east across the river below the falls, switched back west, then east again to a point above the falls. Scattered between trestle and clearing are more remains of the logging kingdom.

Round trip 6 miles
Allow 4½ hours
High point 1120 feet
Elevation gain 880 feet
Best early spring or fall
Gravel road and dirt path

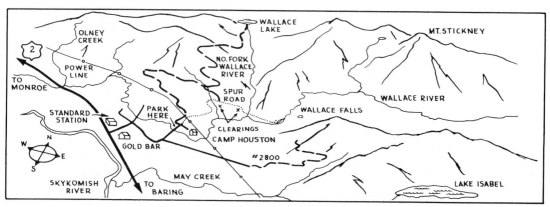

Wallace Falls

Heybrook Lookout, Mount Index, left Mount Persis, right

36   HEYBROOK LOOKOUT

Easy, pleasant, and among the most popular of Northwest mountain hikes. Though Heybrook Lookout is deeper in the hills than most trips in this book, the elevation is low and the route is open road with little wet brush to crowd, so the walk is enjoyable in early spring and early winter, even on rainy days. The road stays close to a Bonneville powerline, which our friend Mr. Bruin, whom we heard grunting from afar, had discovered made an open trail cross-country and naturally preferred to the road with its increasing human traffic. In early spring we encountered no less than a dozen hikers, along with another half-dozen of lazier breed on noisy motorbikes.

Drive US 2 east; pass a roadside rest area at about 3½ miles from Index junction, descend to a railroad bridge, and in about 4 miles from the junction watch for two wooden gates on the left beside the railroad, opposite a house. (The gate farther east has a small sign "Heybrook Lookout.") Park off the highway, NOT in front of the gates or in private driveway. Walk around the gate, cross the railroad, and turn left on gravel road.

In 300 feet or so the level, daisy-edged road turns sharply right and enters woods, climbing gradually. Golden buttercups, Siberian miner's lettuce, and bleeding heart line the way, and maples and alder soon are joined by firs.

The gravel road swings left, then right. The cooling sound of gurgling water rarely ceases as first one, then another, thin stream is met, trickling down the bank and under the road. Wait until just before the 2-mile marker to fill canteens from a more easily accessible pool, where one of the rivulets has been cleared and rocked-in.

Before then, at the 1-mile marker, the road passes under the powerline, parallels it a short distance, crosses under it again and immediately doubles back under the line. Views open up above the line as the way climbs steadily; then woods close in again. At 1½ miles the road levels out for almost a mile. When it reaches the middle of the ridge, it turns northwesterly for the lookout. The 3-mile marker is at another

junction with the powerline. The last mile, slightly downhill, is in the prettiest woods, grown around old stumps holding a lush ground-cover of vanilla leaf and wild ginger. Out of the forest, the road ends at a large clearing on a level knoll, with magnificent views across the Skykomish valley. Mt. Index and Mt. Persis rise above craggy palisades walling off the southwest, and Bridal Veil Falls, seen plunging from high up on the wall, is deceptively needle-thin at this distance.

The 73-foot, prefabricated tower is one of the newest and really modern lookout buildings, easier for the acrophobe to mount than most, and views are more splendid with every step. While you admire the views, admire and envy—if this sort of locale seems inviting—the couple who manned the air-warning station (AWS) here during World War II; 24 hours a day, 12 months of the year. They lived in a "ground house" and did their "spotting" from a shorter tower than the present one.

Round trip 8 miles
Allow 4 hours
High point 1701 feet
Elevation gain 980 feet
Best March through November, often good in winter

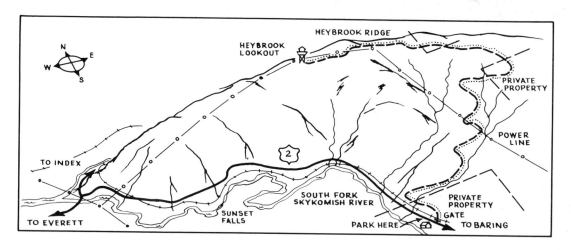

37 LAKE ELIZABETH

It was "your very own Teddy Roosevelt," the Chileans boasted when we traveled through their beautiful lake country, who had called their Lago Todos los Santos (All Saints Lake) the most beautiful in all the world.

All we could say when we saw the lake was that, Teddy Roosevelt hadn't traveled enough of the Northwest, where he could have found many more such jewels. This one, though only 7 acres, is an exquisite emerald mounted in a ring of foothills south of Index.

Drive US 2 east from Sultan 20 miles to Money Creek Campground entrance, just after the town of Grotto and just before entering a highway tunnel. Turn right off the highway and follow paved road past campground and across railroad. In one mile turn right at a Y fork for Lake Elizabeth (No. 2601), and at a second Y in a few feet. The gravel single lane passes between summer cottages, enters woods, crosses a bridge over Money Creek, then it takes off uphill alongside the creek. Now dusty and rocky, the road dances close to look down at the boulder-terraced creek, then away for a look into deep woods. To the south, Lennox Mountain and Bare Mountain rear over the heads of green hills.

At almost 5 miles from US 2, just past a sign marking the elevation as 2000 feet, before the road narrows, park and walk the rest of the way. The lake is just 2¼ miles.

The way levels out then climbs again, but gradually; views down-gorge to the east as the road curves with a hairpin turn. A small cascade plunges across the road about .4 mile from the switchback. Good drinking.

The hiker feels boxed in with the creek; then the road reaches the top of the rise and it is almost a shock to see the tiny, green-blue jewel by the road. Tucked into a pocket of the hills and crimped with a green lace border, the enticing sandy shore and cool water shout "All Yours!" Especially when one hikes in mid-July 90° heat (as I did) and finds not a soul about.

Rest and cool off, then hike another mile to green meadows beyond the lake at road's end, where the Tolt River Watershed begins.

Round trip 4 miles to the lake; 6 miles to road end
Allow 4 hours
High-point 3105 feet
Elevation gain 1105 feet
Best May through October
Gravel road

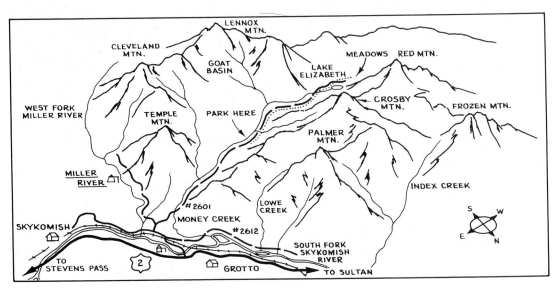

Lake Elizabeth

38   BELLEFIELDS PARK

Visit Bellefields Park for a rare hiking opportunity—that of exploring a marsh where a plant and wildlife community is preserved for study and enjoyment. Once this land was under the waters of Lake Washington, becoming a marsh when the building of the ship canal and locks lowered the lake level.

Go south on 118th Avenue S.E. from Bellevue, or take Highway 405 north or south to Richards Road exit, which intersects 118th. Continue south on 118th exactly 1 mile. At the Bellevue Park Work Yard sign, slow down and park in front of the shop building. Then walk down the road 50 feet to park entrance.

Follow the path to a sign "To Trails" by some huge cedars. A large rectangular area to the right is an old target practice range. The sign, pointing left, leads to Totem Grove—the first of several group-study areas scattered through the park. Park trails total 2½ miles, with rustic signs at all intersections. Strike out in any direction with no fear of getting lost; exit routes are shown everywhere.

Time only for 1 mile, and want it laid out? Here is one pattern: From Totem Grove continue to fork; take right on Mud Lake Boulevard, circle left around Mud Lake, continue past Skunk Cabbage Lane and take right at next three forks—on Fireweed Lane, Alderwood Way, then Cottonwood Avenue. Go left at next two forks—on Maple Way, then the Bee Trail, and rest on a cool, roofed bench straddling a stream at the edge of the old target range, below the parking lot. (This lot is reserved for study groups in advance.)

The trails "float" on spongy peat which reaches a depth of 70 feet in the center. Some places, if one bounces, the earth jiggles! Skunk cabbage as tall as your 7-year-old; marsh grass, alder, cottonwood, patches of sunlit brambles and dark forest; birds by the hundreds and wildlife—muskrat, ducks, skunks, deer, and perhaps even a fox—if you look sharp and sit quietly.

The 48 acres of old Mercer Slough bought by the city with its first park bond issue almost went the usual way of park developments. Plans were made to fill it in for a golf course or grassy picnic ground and ball park. But then Siegfried K. Semrau, Bellevue Park Director, and a few dedicated advisers began to reconsider. Semrau went often to the marsh, early and late in the day, to study its moods.

"One ought not to sit in an office and plan a use, then force your design on the land," he said. "Ask of the land itself what it can do for

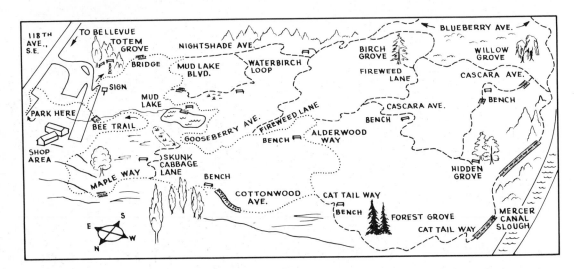

you.'' Semrau and his son even ''played Tarzan'' and jumped from tree to tree to get to the marsh center for a good view.

Later, when the Council was persuaded and plans drafted, Youth Corps boys did much of the work. They swung adzes and machetes, dug with spades and pitchforks, grubbed weeds, cut trees. They worked up to their knees in wet marsh and mud, laid branches, filled in with wood chips, built plank catwalks—and loved it.

Hikers and students long will be grateful for this treat of originality and unusual charm.

Round trip 1 mile to 5
Allow 1 hour or more
Good all year
Plank catwalk or wood-chip trail; may be muddy
and boggy in spots

Mud Lake in Bellefields Park

Jeep road on Squak Mountain

39   SQUAK MOUNTAIN

Issaquah and Squak Mountain are physically and phonetically linked. Physical proximity is apparent at sight—either by map or on foot. Stand in town center and you can hardly miss seeing the mountain. As for the names—a good topic for a linguistic summit conference.

Squak Mountain, a pleasant climb through woods on a road that ascends gradually, then steeply the last half-mile, has been a popular recreation area since white man brought his white sons. Any summer day one may meet—as I did—a youngster riding horseback, munching an apple.

From Issaquah, go west on Sunset Way to a junction with the old Renton Highway (State 900). Continue straight, across highway. Mountain Park Boulevard, our route, turns left uphill, but if one among your party is a tombstone addict, the town cemetery is a few feet straight ahead. Here, overlooking the town, rest many early settlers. Back on Mountain Park Blvd., drive up the steep incline between homes perched on the hillside. In just under a mile the road intersects Mountainside Drive SW. Turn left to the next street, and park on the edge of a dirt road that goes uphill. (Recently gated due to vandalism and patrolled often. Hikers are not prohibited but may be asked their objective.)

The road is a gentle climb for more than a mile, through maple, alder, fir, and cedar that screen the deep gorge alongside. Old moss-grown stumps abound, and a lovely damp pungency pricks the nostrils. Several intriguing side-roads take off here and there, but are better left for later exploring.

Approaching the top is like approaching Heaven—one must work for it! The last ½ mile on old "corduroy" paving is the steepest. Many trees in this last spurt are charred. Six burned trees in a group on the left signal arrival at the top. A few steps farther, on a cleared plateau behind a screen of brush, is the shell of a mountain-top dream house, or perhaps a lodge, badly vandalized. Sadly one contemplates the remnants: a handsome stone fireplace, foot-thick posts, and hundreds of protruding nails from which the ceiling has been ripped.

To the south are a spate of lakes of all sizes between Renton and Maple Valley. Two distant summits of Squak are seen. On the north one is a microwave tower. The road to it, about ¼ mile, branches to the left past the lodge ruins, dips, then ascends to the tower, which offers the best views of the trip.

Over picnic lunch is a good time to practice phonetics. Consider Seattle's founder, Arthur Denny, who wrote in his PIONEER DAYS ON PUGET SOUND: "The name of Squak or Squawk as I would spell it is a corruption of the Indian name of Squowh, or, as some would think to hear the Indians speak it, Isquowh."

Try saying "SSssquowh" bearing down heavily on the hiss. Sounds like EITHER Issaquah or Squak—doesn't it? So the mountain and the town share a name.

Round trip 4 miles
Allow 4 hours
High point 1900 feet
Elevation gain 1700 feet
Good all year, except in deep snow

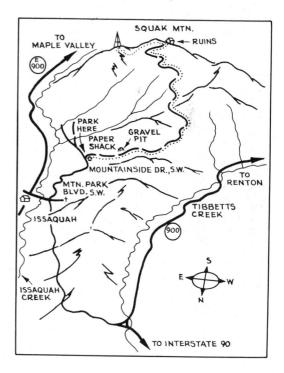

Mount Rainier from Tiger Mountain

40   TIGER MOUNTAIN

Tiger Mountain is a remarkable peak — tallest remnant of a mountain range older than the Olympics and Cascades, rising abruptly and high above impinging suburbs, with views from Rainier to Baker to the Olympics, down to foothills and villages and farms, and into Pugetopolis smog. All within ½ hour of the Lacey V. Murrow Floating Bridge.

Drive Highway 18 (Auburn-North Bend cutoff) 3.3 miles from Issaquah-Hobart Road, or 4.3 miles from I 90, to a low divide. Park on an ample, bulldozed flat by the entrance gate and begin hike uphill on the gravel service road.

The gate has rarely been observed to be closed, and thus it is usually possible to drive to the summit. However, the road is rough and narrow enough to discourage most drivers — and walking, after all, is what this book is about. Let the lazy ones go by in cars; they miss the best fun. But if a party lacks time for the complete hike from the highway, which makes a full afternoon, the road can be driven part way and walked the rest of the way.

Cool, second-growth firs and cedars and hemlocks shade yellow violets, daisies, foxgloves, big-leaf aralia, trillium, and wild ginger, along with tinkling streams. Around a bend into a naked valley and views emerge: Mount Rainier over the shoulder, the lowlands and the Olympics west. At 2½ miles is a junction. Turn right on the bleak sidehill with spectacular views east and south. In ½ mile is a junction with a road from near Preston. More views — from Rattlesnake to Si to Pilchuck to Glacier to Baker. Go left for a final, steep ½ mile to the summit, formerly site of a fire lookout tower, now topped by a microwave facility.

The route lies partly on state-owned land, partly on private. With suburbanites constantly building upwards, little time is left to establish a magnificent Tiger Mountain State Park, including a network of foot and horse trails. (Are the authorities listening?)

Warning: Avoid Tiger Mountain like the plague in hunting season, when murder is legal. An ideal time for the walk is a sunny winter day, when snow stops wheels but not the feet. A spectacular view of city lights can be had after dark, and the sunsets and sunrises are fantastic. Many hikers have spent the night on the summit, carrying water and sleeping bags for a camp.

Round trip from highway 7 miles
Allow 5-6 hours
High point 3004 feet
Elevation gain 1644 feet
Best late fall to early spring — and summer evenings
Gravel road

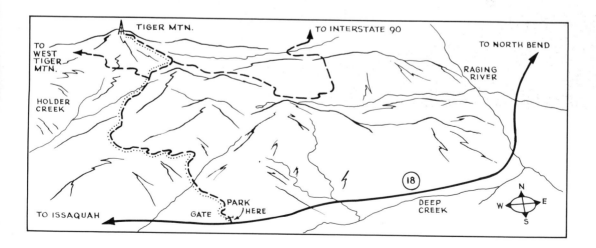

41 WEST TIGER MOUNTAIN

Origins for the name, Tiger Mountain, and its companion, West Tiger Mountain, are varied and vague. A settler named George Tiger? A post-master who came from a town called Tiger in Idaho? Whoever the name-dropper, he must not have seen West Tiger Mountain, for anyone who climbs to the small, open saddle between the two final peaks that rise sharply fore and aft is sure to dub the place Camel Peak. Standing between them, one feels like a rider between the twin humps of a Bactrian camel. From the taller summit are splendid views that sweep a near-circle around Puget Sound from 12 o'clock high to 10 o'clock.

Since West Tiger Mountain is several miles beyond Tiger Mountain, do this walk on a day when the road gate is found to be open. Follow directions for Tiger Mountain, driving to the first main intersection at 2½ miles and parking.

Hike left from the junction. Views over the valley south to Mount Rainier are left behind as the narrow road descends through young trees .8 mile to a T intersection. (To shorten the hike, one can drive to this point and park.) Take the right branch. The level road winds along the base of Tiger and West Tiger, crosses a little creek (water doubtful for drinking), and comes to another fork in about ½ mile; the main road is unmistakable, turning left and beginning a gradual, easy climb.

In ½ mile the road enters a series of hair-pin turns that carry one from terrace to terrace of exhilarating views over a pox of lakes in undulating valleys from Auburn to Kent to Tukwila to Burien to smog-haloed Seattle.

Finally, the camel humps. Rest in the saddle and enjoy a new panorama, stretching north over earth's aquamarine birthmarks of Lake Washington and Lake Sammamish and west across Puget Sound. Then climb the "camel hump" to the right. The last ¼ mile is as steep as an Aztec pyramid — one step at a time! But the effort is worthwhile, climaxing in more views east along the Cascade crest to Rainier in the south. Only the views to the northwest are blocked at the top by the microwave tower and a fringe of greenery.

At the tower, walk downhill to a smaller tower at a lower level. The jeep road curves right behind the second tower; but scout straight ahead in the brush. Here is the end of the popular foot trail from the Preston side — overgrown but still clearly defined, and much used, though legally now "verboten" because it begins on private land.

Round trip 7 miles
Allow 4½ hours
High point 2757 feet
Elevation gain, going and coming, about 1000 feet
Best late fall to early spring — and summer evenings
Gravel road

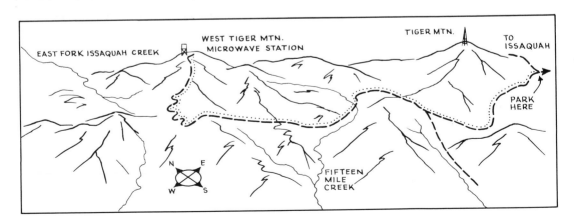

A silver forest near the top of West Tiger Mountain. Tiger Mountain in distance.

42 YELLOWSTONE ROAD

The road is not really yellow. It is red. Paved with red bricks.

From 1910 on, it snaked its way through wild, virgin forests — all the way to Yellowstone National Park. It was the only way to Yellowstone for a long time. Now it is a sentimental thing, linking two highways. Patched here and there with asphalt, it still endures through years of horses, wagons, Model-Ts, modern sedans and trucks. And it probably will go on many more years, though it no longer is the most direct route to Yellowstone Park.

Not often in these days can one hike on a rural road of half-century-old brick. Gather these hikes while ye may — who knows how long the opportunity may stay?

Drive from Redmond southeast on Fall City Highway (State 202) and slow down at the top of a hill about a mile out. At the bottom of the hill, almost another mile, cross a cement culvert bridging Martin Creek. On the other side is 196th Ave. N.E. The blacktop surface is misleading. It covers the beginning of the "Old Red-Brick Road" as Redmond residents call it. Park off the highway shoulder near here and begin the hike. In .1 mile the blacktop disappears to reveal the original brick.

It may be bumpy, it may be old-style, but the rural scenes bordering the road are pure, old-fashioned enchantment. The bricks pace off distance one by one across a level valley over wide beds of rushes bordering Martin Creek, past cattle grazing under a sky quilted with great puffs of cottony clouds. Fragrant thistle and fireweed perfume the road — something only the hiker can enjoy. The bricks flow in a gentle curve right, then left, in a ho-hum, generally northward trend past mailboxes, a few of which have been there since 1921.

In 1.3 miles, the bricks of 196th Avenue end at Union Hill Road, or Dead Man's Corner, called so because of many accidents there. The street continues, but in other paving surface.

On this pioneer state highway that once formed the only link from Seattle to North Bend and points east, the posted speed limit gives pause to reflect.

In Grandma's day, it would have been hair-raising speed. Try it today, over the rough bricks. It still is!

Round trip 2.6 miles
Allow 1¼ hours
Good all year
Road of bricks; bumpy but nostalgic

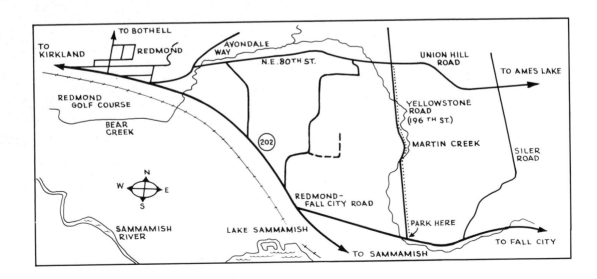

Yellowstone Road

Pussy willow

43   TOLT RIVER PARK

Every hike has its own experience, and each can have its own memory keepsake. Like King County's Tolt River Park — have you ever walked through a dry snowfall?

Still awaiting funds for "development," this park is a small surprise package that may be more enjoyable to the hiker now than later. It provides a ½-mile river walk supplemented by forays into wooded groves here and there, where future improved nature trails are planned to follow existing footpaths already worn by adventurers.

Drive I 90 east and turn north on the Fall City road. Continue north from Fall City on Carnation road (State 203) 4½ miles to the bridge over the Tolt River. A gravel road at the north end of the bridge, marked by a large "County Park" sign, leads to ample parking space under the bridge. Walk west on the gravel riverbank road to the confluence with the Snoqualmie River. The road dwindles to a footpath in woods beyond, but one can continue along the shore when the river is low.

The rushing, gossipy Tolt seems like an energetic youngster as it dances down to join the more sedate, quiet flow of the Snoqualmie. The thick, green fringe on the Tolt's south side adds a wild touch; and wide, wide gravel bars here and there push back the river to invite children to frolic. A hill rising above the junction seems to have been sliced like a loaf of bread by a gargantuan knife. Between the rock strata on the vertical face, trees and greenery struggle for foothold.

At the hill's north end are county park workshop buildings. Park property includes 220 acres on both banks up to the bridge on the main road. Picnic and camp areas, ball fields, and nature trails are planned. The area is a favorite of steelhead fishermen. Waters here are not open to fishing until July since the river is a salmon escapement. In early spring, about May, if the water is very clear, thousands of 5- to 6-inch fingerlings can be seen making their way downriver to the ocean, traveling who knows where? All the way from the series of small peaks squeezed like an accordion between two larger crags in the Cascade ridge framing the bridge on the main road.

The dry snowfall? Make the hike about late May. Just past the junction, stand quietly. Tiny, weightless puffs of gossamer down drift noiselessly to earth from cottonwood trees. Try rubbing a puff between the fingers. Who could wear a gown woven of this frothy filament? Naturally. A wood nymph.

Round trip 1 to 2 miles
Allow 1½ hours
Good anytime; best in spring
Gravel road and sandbars

Highway bridge over Tolt River

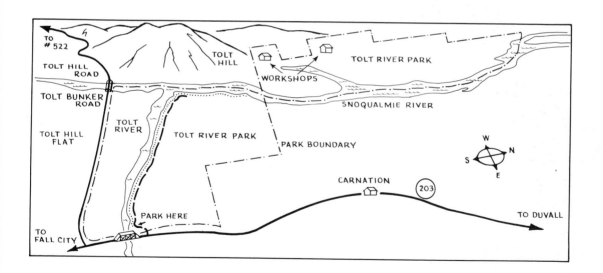

44   LAKE MARIE

In our time, many of the small, dainty lakes of the Northwest within close driving range of Seattle have been all but gobbled up by encroaching humanity. Few such lakes today lack the mushroom "fairy ring" of summer cabins or permanent homes. Ironically, since small lakes will not support more than a few residences with the preordained effluvium, we may also see, in our time, the unpleasant results of these lovely little lakes choked with the burden of civilization's curses.

Lake Marie, only an hour's drive from the big city, is one that still can be seen "au naturel" — steeped in its own natural bog, before the tide of human suction-cups clamps to its shoreline.

From Fall City drive State 202 east toward Snoqualmie Falls. (Coming north from I 90 east of Issaquah, turn to the right in Fall City, just after the bridge.) About 1½ miles, turn left at large sign "Spring Glen Realty." Keep the office and mobile home park on your right, follow the road uphill past residences and across a railroad. Pavement ends and a gravel road continues, winding steeply in a couple of hairpin turns up a steep grade, then through woods where it levels out as a one-lane, smooth dirt road. In about 1½ miles, stick to the right at two succeeding forks. In less than ¼ mile more is a clearing at what appears to be a triple fork. Park here where space is ample.

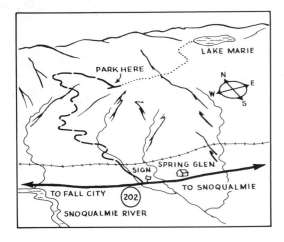

Begin hiking on the narrow dirt track to the left. This walk is usually wet and boggy except in periods of prolonged dry weather. Do NOT attempt to drive in a passenger car. Wear boots or waterproof shoes. The first mudholes may even be seen from the parking place, but pay no mind to the area's sodden aspect. Lake Marie has an eerie, fascinating quality and the effort will seem worth the few mudpuddles. The lane probes through second-growth cedars and firs, spotted with big stumps among ferns and salal. In ½ mile, the track crosses a cleared swath. Over the wide ribbon of stumps and slash glitters a new powerline and towers. On the other side of the powerline an old logging road with a chain barrier branches to the left. Ignore it and continue straight. About 400 paces beyond the powerline, on the left, is an interesting, uprooted tree root system; fully 10 feet high, gnarled and covered with moss. A challenge: Find the trunk stub. Sawed so close to the root mass there appears to be none, one must hunt in the scrub behind to find it. In just under a mile from the powerline is the lake edge, sadly marked by the usual campground litter. Step gingerly on the footpath beyond it, over roots and backwash, to a shoreline view of a mint-julep lake, ringed by reeds, dead snags, and low hills.

Lake Marie's fascination lies in the spongy marshland that encircles it, like an overhanging shelf. Knowledgeable fishermen are not alarmed but expectantly wary when they sink up to ankles and knees as they plod around the lake to the opposite shore. A long string of trout held up to view by one happy angler one July day was reward enough, as far as he was concerned.

And one bright hope remains: that the shelf of sponge fringing the lake may stand off encroaching buildings and keep Lake Marie a green, secluded hideaway.

Round trip 3 miles
Allow 2 hours
High point 953 feet
Good anytime; best in dry summer or when
**   ground is frozen and hard**
Level, dirt jeep road; mudpuddles

Lake Marie

45   SNOQUALMIE FALLS AREA

Though perhaps not the same as that extolled by the popular ballad, our own Snoqualmie is "Moon River." The local Indian "Sdoh-kwahlb-bhuh," as an early-day Tulalip Indian agent tried to record the sounds phonetically, meant "people of the moon." So nothing has really changed much, except now we go TO the moon and still stand in awe of Sdoh-kwahlb-bhuh Falls, girdled by its eternal iris.

This mixture of short hikes in the Falls district that we call a "Sunday afternoon conglomerate" is even better on weekdays, when the sawmill tour can be added.

Drive I 90 east from Issaquah, turn left (north) across highway at sign for Snoqualmie Falls, just west of North Bend. Immediately after turning is a fork. Take the right (394th Place Southeast) marked "Snoqualmie Falls."

Keep straight past the next intersection and follow the small green Weyerhaeuser signs past Mount Si High School, over a bridge, under a railroad trestle, and a couple of left turns at forks. Follow the uphill road above the plant buildings as directed by a sign, for a Tree Farm and Sawmill Tour. The mill tours begin at 10 a.m. and 1:30 p.m. Monday through Friday.

The former Nature or Ecology Trail which provided a pleasant ½-mile hike through a miniature tree farm, with mounted explanations about the trees' life struggles, has been closed off. However, a new trail is under development farther down the road. Ask at the tour office if it is ready for visitors.

For the next part of the conglomerate, leave the mill and return to the railroad trestle. Turn right on Millpond Road, which leads to the highway in front of Snoqualmie Falls Lodge. A "posh" trail to the right of the snack bar in Puget Sound

Air view of Snoqualmie Falls during spring run-off

Power and Light's park coasts steeply down ½ mile to a powerhouse above the river. On the return, branch right to the cantilevered viewing platform for a bird's-eye view of the 270-foot falls. The volume of water varies from a thick wall in spring to thin plumes in fall, but always impressive in height.

Now drive west from the Lodge a mile to a gated road on the right. CAUTION: Since first publishing, Weyerhaeuser's Tokul Creek Park area has been leased to a gun club for target practice, for an undetermined time, so check if gun club sign is on gate. If shots are heard (park can be seen below highway) it may be wiser to avoid this part until later. Or if planning a picnic, call Snoqualmie Valley Rifle Club for target meet dates. The gravel road goes to picnic tables beside a burbling stream in Tokul Creek Park. Park and cross the sturdy log bridge. A trail climbs gradually above the creek about ¾ mile to deadend at a county road.

For the final polish on the conglomerate, drive a few yards farther west on the highway to the Tokul Creek Fish Hatchery, where millions of trout fingerlings are produced yearly by the State Game Department. A path leads from the buildings and outside tanks to other holding tanks at riverside level, adding a long flight of steps to the hike.

Round trip (all hikes) 3½ miles
Allow 3½ hours
Good all year
Dirt, gravel, and brick-dust paths

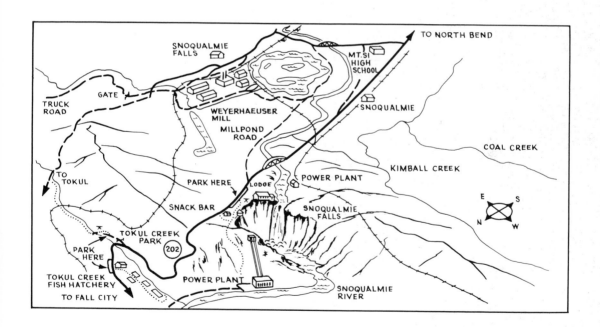

46 SNOQUALMIE FALLS — WEST SIDE

Every resident and tourist sees our Snoqualmie Falls from the easy vantage point provided by the modern "space platform." Try a new approach: that of an explorer.

Imagine tagging along with Colonel J. Patton Anderson of the US Infantry, and his companion, Lieutenant Floyd Jones, as they explore along the river in July, 1852. One white man before them had seen and told of the falls, and the story has drawn the two men into the country of the "moon people" to see their mystic, liquid moon-bolt.

Drive I 90 east about 5 miles east of Issaquah to Preston and turn left (north). Continue to Fall City, but do not cross the bridge on entering town. (Or, if there is time left in the day and this tour is being added to the "Snoqualmie conglomerate," Hike 45, continue west from Tokul Creek Fish Hatchery across the Snoqualmie River bridge to Fall City. Then cross a steel bridge over Raging River at the south edge of town.)

Turn east at south end of bridge on David Powell Road which follows the river. At 2.3 miles, where road turns right uphill is a parking area. Property here is owned by Snoqualmie Falls Forest Theater, a non-profit cultural group and hikers, while welcome, may find parking space unavailable during their summer fairs, concerts and forest theater performances. July through September are busiest months if you plan to hike only; but for complete family-day fun combine the walk with one of their popular steak barbecues and outdoor productions.

Pick up the path going east from parking area. It continues through willows, brush and berry bushes to the viewpoint.

Almost from the beginning a dull throb is an undercurrent to the hike. With each step the noise swells until it assumes a muffled roar, and suddenly, there it is.

This tiny viewpoint at the edge of a precipice gives a sight of the falls far more thrilling, though more distant, than that from the "tourist" station. One almost snickers at the figures of viewers seen on the luxurious platform on the opposite side of the river. They have not "discovered" the Great Falls of the Moon People from the primitive, undeveloped side.

Since first writing, a diligent Boy Scout Troop has added a bench and extended the trail

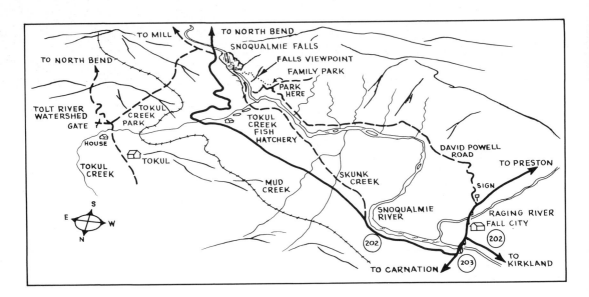

Snoqualmie Falls from viewpoint on west-side trail

from the viewpoint down to the river's edge. Here was a neutral zone, where Indians of many tribes camped for powwows and to write peace treaties in the sand, anointed, as you now are, by spray from the falls.

Round trip 2 miles
Allow 1½ hours
Good all year but crowded
June through September
Dirt-and-gravel path

47 FULLER MOUNTAIN LAKES

Fuller Mountain, trying to emulate its big brother, Mount Si, rises in a single hump out of a valley 5 miles northeast of Snoqualmie Falls. It stands guard over three peaceful lakes, dangling in a north-south string on its west flank. The fun of this hike is to watch Fuller Mountain move as you pull yourself along the string, from lake to lake. Set aside an entire day and begin

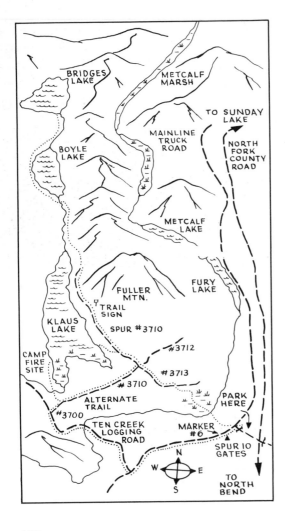

early, as this is a semi-rugged hike, but one with a great range of Nature's treats — deep woods, marshes, and primitive lakes.

Drive I 90 east to North Bend. Turn left on Ballarat Street 2 blocks east of stoplight. Go through town on North Fork County Road to Weyerhaeuser's Spur 10 gate. Double gates bar parallel logging roads east and west. Park in area provided by the west gate. Take picnic lunch, water, and emergency items. The trail is distinct but CAN be missed!

From the west gate walk south about 75 feet. Find a trail into woods across the road from a small yellow company mile-marker, No. 6. In 200 yards, left of a big tree, is a series of logs and planks over deep-green, moss-lined pools. Watch your step! The logs are slippery.

The path climbs slightly from low marshland, past moss-covered logs and stumps and in ½ mile drops 2 feet onto logging road No. 3713 that follows an old railroad bed. Turn left. Old stumps, ferns, moss, Oregon grape, wildflowers, and mushrooms in season cover the forest floor between big trees, now being thinned by the company. About ½ mile from Spur 10 Gate another logging road (3710) swings in from the left to join yours (now also No. 3710). Mark it mentally as an alternate route for return. (It actually crosses your road but becomes 3712 as it continues to the right.)

Fuller Mountain appears over trees to the right as the path edges swampy pools, then seems to come up almost beside the hiker, looming so close over a grove of alder and cottonwoods that marks of rock slides can be seen.

Nearly a mile from Spur 10 Gate, watch for a side-trail to the left around a small hill. Follow the left branch 200 yards to the east shore of Klaus Lake, roomier and more pleasant for picnic lunch than the lakes farther north. Klaus is the largest (62 acres) of the three.

Return to the trail fork and continue on the road north. It snakes ¾ mile through open forest, climbing gradually in and out of big tree stands. Soon the road ends and only the railroad grade is left. The path dips to a log bridge over a stream draining 24-acre Boyle Lake. Surrounded by tall reeds and cattails, the lake begets an eerie, lonesome feeling. Fuller Mountain now is seen to the southeast. Scout left through brush

Boyle Lake and Fuller Mountain

for the trail north ¾ mile more to Bridges Lake, 34 acres.

The alternate route mentioned for the return follows another old railway line and adds 2 miles. About ⅝ mile after leaving the lakes route, the road forks. Turn left on Ten Creek Logging Road (3700). (If you want to explore farther the right fork leads over Ten Creek and through woods to the west shore of Klaus Lake.) In ¾ mile is the junction with the mainline road from Spur 10 Gate. Left again ½ mile is the parking area.

Round trip 2½ miles; with alternate return, 4½ miles
Allow 4-6 hours
High point 1045 feet
Elevation gain 65 feet
Best April to October; often possible in winter. Avoid hunting season.
Trail and roads; swampy and muddy areas

48   LAKE HANCOCK

Like aquamarine buttons studding the lapel of a green tunic topping the western rim of the Cascade range are its many small lakes, with larger Lake Hancock and its companion, Calligan, standing out like sapphire lavalieres.

The way to Lake Hancock is a steady climb by open road through logged-over land. Not so bleak and desolate as it sounds: views west expand with each terrace attained; newly-planted trees fill in between bleached stumps and everywhere is a quickening of life under a canopy of blue sky. But begin early on hot days, in the cool of the morning. Take a picnic lunch. Canteens can be filled at a cascade near the end of the hike.

Drive US 10 east to North Bend. Turn left (north) on North Ballarat Street, thence out of town on North Fork County Road about 7½ miles to Weyerhaeuser's Spur 10 double gate. Park there and walk up the east road (No. 10), bearing left until it meets No. 13 at junction with No. 11. Continue on No. 13. Beginning at a hairpin turn

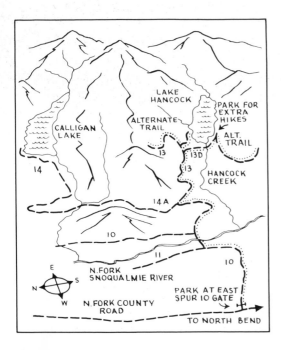

beside cascading Hancock Creek, views from one switchback to another up the mountainside are like adding sections to an aerial map. The imposing, rounded hump of Fuller Mountain dwindles in perspective with tributaries flowing into the Snoqualmie River; lakes dot the plain west to Lakes Sammamish and Washington and Puget Sound.

For a break, climb a huge stump by the road and count the rings — some total more than 400 years. At a fork about 1 mile, go straight (sign "⅞"). At the next fork, 1¼ miles, Spur 14A departs abruptly left to climb around the nearby hill (branch road to Calligan Lake). Keep straight. Follow yellow-paint guide marks on boulders or tree stumps at four more forks or, if faded, a simple guide: go left, then right, then straight (third fork is three-pronged). At the last fork the lake can be seen at the end of a stub to the right. Deep, blue, dramatic, one can almost expect Wagner's Valkyries riding on the clouds over the rocky peaks beyond.

The hike from the gate is best on a weekday, when traffic is lighter. Two alternate, steep hikes yielding smashing views high above the lake are possible but take extra energy; they can, however, be done by driving to the lake. Weyerhaeuser opens the gate as often as possible. With a few exceptions, when operations are necessary or during fire hazard, Spur 10 gate is open Saturdays and Sundays, beginning April 15 from 6 a.m. to 9 p.m. From October 15 through December 15 the gate is closed earlier, at 6 p.m. (Watch the time or prepare to spend a night locked in!) Hiking on weekends is not recommended. Traffic is heavy and the road is very dusty, especially during hunting and fishing season. (When hunters prowl the slopes, stay away. We have felt in dire peril with shots popping on all sides.)

For the two extra hikes, drive to the three-pronged, third fork mentioned above and turn right on 13D, a logging spur (actually a few yards ahead of the other two). Cross Hancock Creek bridge and park. The level road follows the south shore of the lake a short distance, then abruptly climbs after a sharp turn. In ½ mile it rises nearly 500 feet; magnificent views reach far to the west as well as to the lake below. Return to the fork, park and follow the left

Lake Hancock from logging road No. 13D

branch (13) which climbs above the lake's north side. Views increase as one mounts, with best views in 1 mile. The steep west face of Mount Si is unmistakable south of the lake. Far below, flocks of ducks coast happily on cobalt wavelets of their own spacious, private pond — all 236 acres of it.

Round trip from gate 6 miles;
   two alternates, 3 miles total
Allow 4½ hours; 2½ hours extra for alternates
High point 2172 feet; 2672 feet
Elevation gain 2012 feet; 2512 feet
Best April to October; good often earlier and later

49　SUNDAY LAKE

The only thing wrong with Sunday Lake is its name. A perfect lake; a perfect family hike. But why only Sunday? Better "Any Day Lake." We started early one Saturday and on the return hike met three families.

This small turquoise bowl, fringed with firs, is not too deep in the mountains; the 4-mile climb makes a pleasant outing, possible much later in fall and earlier in spring than most.

Drive I 90 east to North Bend. Turn left on Ballarat Street, 2 blocks east of first stop light. Later it becomes the "North Fork County Road." At a fork about 4 miles, go straight, uphill (Lake Hancock sign). Pavement ends just after fork. In 5 more miles, the gravel road passes

Sunday Lake

116

Weyerhaeuser's double "Spur 10 Gate," and in another 10 miles is "Spur 30," another gate for an intersecting logging road. (Previous sign "Sunday Lake" may be gone.) Park on shoulder well away from gates and begin hike on road going southeast. Warning: If gate is open, do not enter in car. Drivers often are locked in overnight when logging trucks return early.

The pebbled, sandy road cuts through open clearcut area, covered with bleached stumps, slash, scrub growth, and young, hand-planted seedlings. It makes a wide curve right, then aims for low foothills to the southeast. At a Y in 1 mile bear right below a spur road that ascends steeply to the left. In about ½ mile more the road widens into another Y. The right is only an access to the gravel bars of musical Sunday Creek. Keep left, slightly uphill here, and at a couple more access roads to the creek farther on. At 2 miles, the road dips to a new, cedar log bridge. Cross it and turn left. A National Forest marker in the next half mile marks the trail to the lake.

Since first writing, a section of forest has been clearcut, but big trees fortunately remain in the upper half of the trail. Aged Western red cedars and Douglas firs prompt the quote: "This is the forest primeval . . ."

The trail levels out to smooth ground about a mile from the bridge, then climbs again. Big rocks and boulders draw more exertion on the last and steepest ½ mile. Several big mudholes may require slight detours. At the top of an open knoll the trail feathers out into several directions. A splinter of metallic blue, 30 feet down the slope, strikes the eye. The shore is reached easily — an inviting gravel bar and dead snags at one end for youngsters' frolic and thickly-wooded banks surrounding for adult exploration. (Much more inviting from a distance than the fishermen's campsite at hand, made ugly with litter.)

Sunday Lake, a favorite with trout fishermen, is 21.2 acres. To the left, behind the gravel bar, is tiny adjacent Lower Sunday Lake, 2.3 acres. The trail continues beyond, heading south into the mountains for Mowitch Lake, but that is another 4-mile story.

Round trip 7 miles
Allow 5½ hours
High point 1865 feet
Elevation gain 317 feet
Best March to November; often good in winter
Gravel road and dirt trail

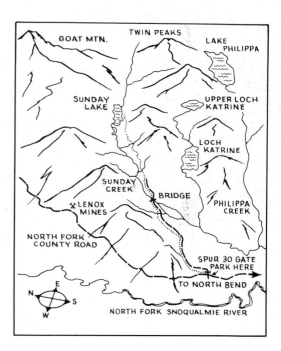

Mount Garfield, the rugged peak at the big bend of the Middle Fork Snoqualmie River, from Green Mountain

*pleasant drive & hike
moderate climb
woods poor — good scenery*

50 GREEN MOUNTAIN (NORTH BEND)

Map-browsing can be more fun than anything. Pick a spot that looks intriguing. Follow it up. The phrase "mining claims" on a map nipped us. We followed the dangling teaser (a steady, uphill climb; not for complainers) to a high, windy hill and hung there, mesmerized by splendid views. Back at our doorstep, we remembered. The mining claims? We never got there. But who needs them? The reward is a panorama of unusual views into Snoqualmie back country.

Drive east from North Bend on I 90 about 1 mile. Turn left on 432nd S.E. (Stilson Road) and cross the westbound traffic lane. The same road now is marked "Mt. Si Road." Follow it across a railroad and bridge over the Middle Fork of the Snoqualmie River, where it turns east. In a mile from the highway it is marked "Forest Service Road" and at 3½ miles pavement ends. A sign here cautions "Not Recommended for Passenger Cars." A "Road Closed" sign also may be posted, routing traffic to a new road south, but climb with caution on the narrow, rough road through close woods along a ravine to a fork at 3.2 miles. (Only an iron post remains of a former sign which pointed straight ahead for Camp Brown and Taylor River Campground. That road now is impossible.) Turn left on an uphill gravel lane and drive ¼ mile to a wide gravel pit, where the road forks. Park here and begin hiking on the right fork. (Do not try to drive.)

In early spring, bleeding heart, yellow violets, Siberian miner's lettuce, and star-flowered Solomon's Seal border the rocky road as it climbs gradually at first, over bad rocks and holes, then more steeply, compensating in a mile with smoother surface. Leafy alders and maples among the few drooping hemlocks and cedars keep the hiker cool the first ½ mile. The close growth darkens the hillside below the trail but among their trunks can be seen huge old moss-grown stumps and logs. In 1½ miles a series of sharp, rocky switchbacks slows the pace, but at each hairpin turn the views of peaks east and north draw the puffing laggards on.

One foot at a time, now; no hurry! Stop where the road splits, ending on the left in a big logging slash pile and continuing around a sharp

bend to the right, beyond a hiker's interest. Five minutes more to the right and a large, flat viewpoint. Here is the ocular banquet of the day. A succession of peaks marches along the skyline beyond the vast valley — rugged Garfield Mountain north; next, the rounded slopes of Preacher Mountain, then Russian Butte, a series of rugged peaks across the valley directly opposite. South of the Butte is Grouse Ridge, and peering over a ridge to the south, ubiquitous Mount Rainier. Through the deep valley the metallic silver thread of the Snoqualmie's Middle Fork embroiders the land, snaking its way between Mt. Garfield and Russian Butte, then turning southwest to run under your toes. A picnic lunch has a magnificent flavor here. (But carry water; there's little along the way.)

Green Mountain belies its name. The road was built to log state-owned timber on the upper slopes, and it may be a long time before the mountain is wholly green again.

Round trip 5 miles
Allow 4 hours
High point 3200 feet
Elevation gain 1700 feet
Best May through October

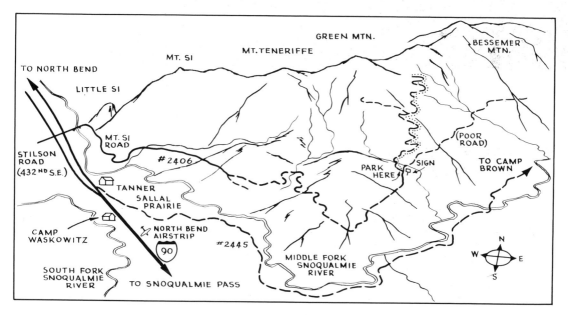

A winter's day on the Tolt Park Pipeline Park Trail.

51   TOLT PIPELINE PARK TRAIL

Happiness is being able to bounce out your back door right onto a trail and walk for miles over hill and dale, as I saw one large family do on this hike.

The Tolt Pipeline service road from Bothell to the Snoqualmie River, which so far as public use was concerned long seemed a virtual "pipe dream," now has been dedicated as the first King County trail in a hoped-for state-wide network. The 12 miles of the Seattle Water Department right-of-way initially were converted to recreational use with voter approved Forward Thrust funds and improvements constantly are being added by King County Department of Parks. Future plans include bridges over freeway, road, and river; restrooms; and divided trails for hikers and/or horsemen and bicyclists.

Beginning and end are not yet completed. Directions are given here for accessible portions, where the trail is well signed and gated at road crossings.

Officially the trail starts near Wayne Golf Course, skirts Bothell's Blyth City Park, and climbs a steep hill to 104th Avenue NE. One could presently begin at 104th, with a magnificent view of Seattle and the Olympic Mountains. (Drive south from Bothell over Sammamish River Bridge and south from Riverside Drive on 102nd Avenue NE, which merges with 104th. At about 1 mile, park near marked trail gate, close to NE 162nd Street.) This first 2-mile portion goes downhill from the view (one brief, steep drop) and runs into I-405 —which is not only very dangerous to cross, but illegal.

For a longer and equally pleasant hike, the practical starting point is east of I-405. Exit from freeway at NE 160th Street (south of Bothell exit) and turn south from exit on 116th Avenue NE. In less than ¼ mile park by the signed trail gate easily seen behind a row of homes.

The well-worn footpath centered in the graveled service road starts on a level between houses and trees that reverse sides before the trail crosses 119th Avenue NE and goes gently downhill. It begins a gradual ascent after crossing 124th

Avenue NE, climbing to another good view of cities and mountains. Across the dirt stub-end of 132nd Avenue NE the trail drops steeply, with views along the way over the valley, to the Woodinville-Redmond Road edging the Sammamish River.

Until a bridge is built, one must detour south to the NE 145th Street bridge. Pick up the trail following the river bank north, or continue on 145th to 148th Avenue NE and north to trail sign. Either detour adds 1 mile. From 148th the trail climbs steeply, then detours north to NE 153rd Street to avoid a steep bank. A bridge may eliminate the detour soon. Signs mark the return to the pipeline (and the only place the water pipe is actually seen) at 155th Avenue NE.

From there another climb between scattered houses and pastures leads to a panoramic view of Seattle city skyscrapers and Olympic Mountains. Across 168th Avenue NE, the way descends through forest past the Brookside Golf Course and makes three quick highway crossings, the last being Mink Road (206th Avenue NE).

From Mink Road, after a few houses, the trail enters a 3-mile section of primitive forest, crosses several forest roads, reaches another Snoqualmie Valley viewpoint, then descends steeply to the present trail-end on the West Snoqualmie Valley Road.

At this eastern end, parking currently is extremely limited.

Round trip 20 miles (between 116th Avenue and Duvall end)

Allow 1 to 8 hours (for sections or total)

Good anytime — wet in places in winter

Gravel path

Fog-filled Snoqualmie Valley and 5535-foot McLain Peak from Tolt Pipeline Park Trail.

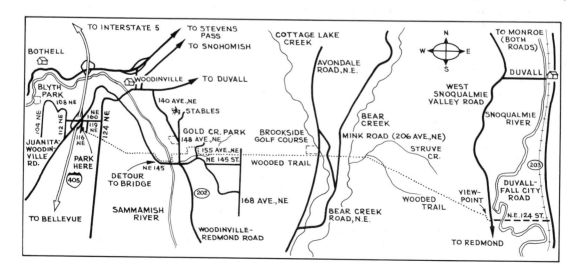

52 RATTLESNAKE MOUNTAIN

Rattlesnakes are not to be found west of the Cascades. So it is with a puzzled air one finds a massive mountain ridge of such name between Issaquah and North Bend. We'll savor the answer with the views when we've reached the top.

Drive I 90 east toward North Bend. Slow down after crossing over the Auburn cutoff (Highway 18) and watch carefully for a gravel service road — hidden until one is on top of it — on the right (south) side about 1½ miles from Highway 18. The entrance widens in a small apron with room to park. Leave the car here. The road narrows and becomes quite rough for driving, but is an instant nature walk, ascending gradually (road may be muddy after heavy rains) through alder, big leaf maple, hemlock, cedar, and firs. A gorge deepens on the left as the road gets steeper and the woods thicker. Old stumps are screened with lattices of ferns and devil's club. At about 1½ miles from the highway the road reaches a powerline and divides.

Two possibilities from here: label them "Men" and "Mice." For Men, take a good breath and charge up the steep, loose-graveled road to the right. It ends near the top in ½ mile. Walk back about 200 feet to the first tower for the best view. When breath is regained, the views regale.

One can stand for long minutes and feast on this banquet of sights. A sweeping view of North Bend, dominated by Mount Si. The Middle Fork of the Snoqualmie River (deceivingly sluggish from this height) curls lazily in front of Mount Si and north to meet its brother, the North Fork. The powerline marches east across hill and dale. To the south, Mount Washington rears above Chester Morse Lake.

For Mice, not quite as lofty views, but still impressive, are possible by taking the more level, easier hike on the left branch from the fork beside the powerline. In ½ mile the road dips to another fork under powerline towers. Stop here and go no farther. The Bonneville Power Administration would like to accommodate hikers along its powerline, but legally are prevented. They have easements from private property owners only to erect and service the line. Any casual traveler must obtain his own permission or easement. Views from here, over North Bend, Mount Si, the Cascades north and south, the river, and Mount Washington are almost as good for those satisfied at being Mice.

As for rattlesnakes on the mountain, Arthur Denny, pioneer Seattle founder, tells us:

"One of the party (of pioneer road surveyors) was startled by a rattling in the weeds. He reported that he heard a rattlesnake, which on investigation proved to be simply the dry seed pods of a weed; but it was sufficient to give a name to the place which it has ever after kept."

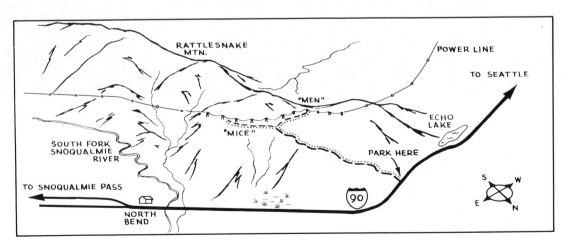

North Bend and Mount Si from Rattlesnake Mountain

Round trip, Men or Mice, 4 miles
Allow 3 hours
High point: Men, 2500 feet; Mice, 2000 feet
Elevation gain: Men, 500 feet
Good all year except in snow
Gravel road

53 FRANKLIN FALLS

When it comes to waterfalls, the Northwest runneth over.

Many long-time residents are unaware of the wealth of cataracts, each as individual as a fingerprint, within a few hours' reach. If one could collect and mount them, they'd make a gallery of flowing masters, no two alike.

It's hard to choose a favorite. But the walk to Franklin Falls is a woodland idyl — and a teaser. It's the surprise element that "grabs."

Drive I 90 about 17 miles east of North Bend. Turn left at sign for Denny Creek Campground and continue east on paved road 2 miles. Park inside campground and walk north ¼ mile to the road and a fork. Left a few steps is the trail marked "Franklin Falls" at a bridge over the South Fork of the Snoqualmie River.

Big cedars and firs convoy the hiker beside the singing stream on a wide, needle-paved path, their roots a sprawling web for unwary feet. One huge cedar snag leans wearily against a hemlock, the two trunks seemingly one. Chanterelle mushrooms (in season) hide in mossy pockets among old trees; devil's club skulks in the background behind vine maple, berry bushes, graceful deer fern, bunchberry, False Solomon's Seal, and skunk cabbage bordering the path.

In ½ mile the path bores into the gorge, now climbing in earnest. Views are 40 feet down to racing water splashing from boulder to boulder and surging around a 150-foot-long fallen giant that has plunged its top into midstream. A massive granite boulder opposite, big as a house, shows tempting glimpses of caves.

Rustic bridges cross feeder rivulets and railings appear where the cliff edges, now 60 feet above rapids, come dangerously near. The soft, mossy turf springs back from the tread like foam-rubber. A road appears suddenly on the right (the old Snoqualmie Pass Highway) but the trail ducks back into woods. Up-gorge, to the left, a thin plume of water comes into view, dangling from a high, rocky cliff. Eyes trained on the high, thin cascade, a hiker wonders how it can make the muted roar now heard above the noisy creek.

Wild lily-of-the-valley

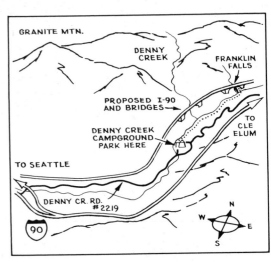

He rounds a projecting cliff face; his face is bathed in misty spray and he stops, jaw agape. After the deluding handkerchief-size spume, this looks like Niagara Falls! (Modern "progress" has added its brand; a new highway bridge spans the top.)

The cataract is an intimate sort. Water hurls itself down the rocky precipice 75 feet into a heavenly pool, hesitates and swirls under a rainbow arc, as though reluctant to go on, then spills over a sandy rim to join the downward dance. Such a pool few can resist, and since the trail is not as high above-gorge here, inch down the rocky ledge carefully (the alternative is a slide) to the pool.

Then wade. Dodge the wild waters in a hilarious shower. Or perch on a rock and dream.

Round trip 3 miles
Allow 1½ hours
High point 2500 feet
Elevation gain 280 feet
Best June to October
Forest path

Franklin Falls in June

Tahuya Lake, Hood Canal, and Olympic Mountains from Green Mountain

54 GREEN MOUNTAIN (BREMERTON)

Of all the redundancies in our lovely Evergreen State, it's the plenitude of "Green Mountains." But this one apparently came by the name legitimately, honoring the memory of William K. Green, an early landowner. Anyway, this green hill is one of the easiest and prettiest hikes west of Puget Sound. Since this book was first written, the state has built a new access road from the west, and plans more recreational improvements, including a horse camp, riding and hiking trails.

Take cross-Sound ferry to Bremerton, turn right from dock to Washington Avenue and left at signal light on Sixth Street, which then merges into four-lane highway (State 3). Turn left at sign for Seabeck, almost 4 miles, then follow signs through several turns for Lake Symington, about 8 miles. (This route also is marked for The Mountaineers' Forest Theater.) Just past the marked lake entrance road and the lake itself, turn left on Lake Tahuyeh Road. In less than a mile, turn left on a road marked "Green Mt. Vista."

The gravel road ascends through a veritable florist shop of ferns, salal, Oregon grape, spirea, and rhododendrons, lovely in bloom. Numerous signs state "No brush picking." (The lands are leased by professional brush-pickers.) The sun plays a game of tag with its shadow among gray-white alders.

In just under a mile the road swings right to meet the old service road. Go right, uphill, 3/4 mile. Where the road levels momentarily, watch for wet marshy plants of a beaver pond on the left. Turn left on a side road here and park where there is room off the road, to begin the hike. The main road starts climbing again and forks in 1/4 mile at a sharp right turn. The left leads to a new horse camp. Keep right. About 1/2 mile from the fork, pass a spur road going left downhill just before a sharp right turn. Walk straight between the spur and the right turn, on a seldom-used narrow road that bores through a wall of second-growth forest. A small rock quarry appears; just before it, turn right and climb back to the main road for the last 1/4-mile steep climb to the top.

The original tower lookout, maintained since 1928, was removed when replaced by aerial fire detection. Only the supports remain.

Views are like long draughts of heady liquor. Tahuya Lake, Hood Canal, and Olympics to the west; monster cranes of Bremerton and the Navy Yard, Port Orchard, Puget Sound, and Cascades to the east. Even Seattle's Space Needle!

Picnic tables and conveniences will be installed about the time this book goes to print, for day use only. Overnight camping will be permitted at the horse camp.

Round trip 2½ miles
Allow 2 hours
High point 1639 feet
Elevation gain 439 feet
Best March to October; often good earlier and later
Dirt and gravel road

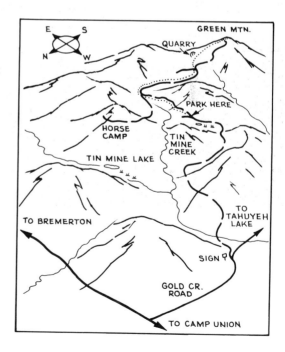

55   FORT WARD

Nothing is sadder than to see a dead colony: a complex of abandoned buildings; a compound of wide, green lawns overlooking blue waters; backyards still showing worn areas where once children laughed and played. A walk there can be poignant, among whispering ghosts. Fort Ward is like that.

Still, this 480-acre wooded hillside, sloping to a long, 1½-mile strip of beach facing Rich Passage, is ideal for hiking.

Take cross-Sound ferry to Winslow. From ferry dock leave Hood Canal Bridge Highway and go through Winslow center to Madison Avenue North. Turn right on Madison and left at next intersection, on Wyatt Way Northwest. Follow signs straight through Lynnwood Center, about 2½ miles. About .6 mile is a Y fork.

Here is a choice: the left, uphill, marked "South Beach," leads to the fort's "top gate," via blacktop road and a right turn in about a mile. Fort Ward signs clearly mark the way after this fork.

For the sea level west gate, follow the right branch of the Y ½ mile to the entrance gate and park just inside. Leave the car and follow the narrow lane under big maples and madronas as it undulates gently, as though on swells from the sparkling water in the strait alongside. In ½

mile it comes out of the woods onto a cleared strip beside two large barracks buildings perched just above shoreline. A state parks recreation area is being developed here at this writing.

Continue past the buildings and walk around a road barrier. A few steps beyond are old emplacements where guns were trained across Rich Passage to protect Bremerton Navy Yard. The dingy concrete pillbox, scrunched among weeds, seems even more desolate under the lonely sound of a bell buoy ringing from afar. During World War II, submarine nets were strung from here clear across Rich Passage. Now the pillbox looks only at the ubiquitous Mount Rainier, shimmering across dancing whitecaps of the smoke-blue Sound.

Do not walk farther — it becomes private property at the old, Sunset Lodge a few yards on, and besides, poison oak festoons the roadway! Return to the parked car and follow directions given to the "top gate." Park there and walk along "Main Street," where extensive brick buildings still wear the military look, down to the pier at shore level. The shore walk eastward ends at private property in .2 mile.

For a delightful lagniappe in another tiny pocket of the fort area, return to the car and the Y fork. Take the left branch, but do not follow the right turn sign for Fort Ward's top gate; continue straight (Rockaway Beach sign) for .2 mile. Where a spur dips right to an old brick building,

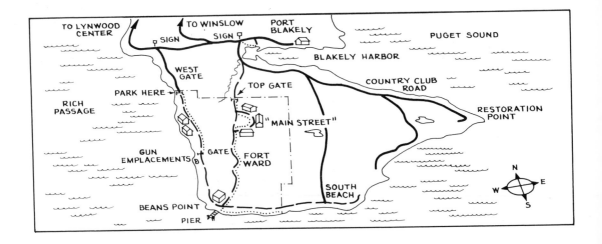

Cormorants at Fort Ward

park and walk out to an intriguing lagoon filled with logs. A worn truck and crane still in service may be standing beside an old shed. Circle around the shed and return to the car, or if the ghosts are whispering, sit on a log among the blackberry bushes, yarrow, and buttercups and listen to wild canaries sing.

Fort Ward was established in 1891 to protect the Bremerton Navy Yard. But it was always a "gonna be," remaining in limbo, a patch of woods, until officially designated in 1903 and named in honor of Colonel George H. Ward, who died at Gettysburg. Six years later the federal machinery stirred; buildings were erected and guns installed. But in 2 years, even while buildings were under construction, the fort was placed on inactive status and returned to limbo until used as a children's camp. During World War II the Navy installed a radio training school. In 1956 the Army suddenly reappeared. After a few months the Navy moved out. (No comment.) In 1958 the Army vacated the fort that never really was.

Round trip 3.8 miles
Allow 3 hours
Good all year
Paved road

56   SUQUAMISH

Every Puget Sounder with a sense of history should visit the final resting place of our Great Red Father — Chief Seattle, or Sealth, friend of the first white settlers, elected chief of six tribes. No one can fail to respect him for his regal bearing, his sincerity, his superb oratory; or to realize the anguish and torment of decision it was his tragic destiny to endure. Chief Seattle sleeps peacefully, we hope, in a cemetery not far from the longhouse in which he lived. Our hike goes from one to the other in much shorter span of time than the 80 years of the old chief.

Take cross-Sound ferry to Winslow and drive

Chief Sealth's grave

State 305 about 6½ miles from ferry dock to Agate Pass Bridge. Cross bridge and turn right at north end, on side-road marked for Suquamish. A tall, colorful totem pole, facing the sea, first is seen as the road dips down to town center, 1½ miles. Park in the small plaza below and begin the hike at the pole, which was carved by one of the Northwest's best-known Indian carvers, Joe Hillaire, for the Seattle World's Fair.

Walk up the street right of the pole toward steepled St. Peter's church half a block above. Behind the church is the Memorial Cemetery. A granite shaft, enclosed by a fence, sits apart under the protective branches of a huge, spreading tree. Read its sobering inscription. Chief Seattle. Born in 1786. Wander among the other Indian graves. Intriguing names and mementos mark the panels and stones dotting the green turf. One obelisk-shaped stone is dedicated to the wives of one man — all three named Mary. Another marks the grave of the last chief of the Suquamish tribe, who died at the age of 112.

From the cemetery, return to the street and continue right, uphill. At Division Street, next block, go left across the main highway and continue walking the paved road as it makes a wide curve left, .3 mile, down to the shore road. Turn left, uphill, to the Old Man House, a State Parks and Recreation Commission archeological site, a few steps farther, at the top of a steep bank, where a sign briefly describes the longhouse where Chief Seattle lived. Follow the serpentine footpath down the grassy slope, but do not ignore the exhibit of the hand-adzed cedar slabs similar to those used in roofing the largest known Indian house in the Puget Sound region. Continue the path to the gravelly beach.

Disappointed? Nothing remains but tiny bits of seashells on a rounded point. But sit on a driftwood chunk, gaze across Agate Pass to the opposite point, as the old chief might have done, and let the years roll back. Here stood a magnificent structure, 520 feet long, 60 feet wide, 15 feet high in front. A slanted roof of those cedar slabs just seen was supported by 74 split timbers carved with figures. Logs 65 feet long and a foot thick formed the cross beams; outside walls were split cedar planks. Inside, they partitioned 40 apartments. On corner posts of the chief's apartment were carved great thunderbirds.

Make the return trip by beach, if the tide is right. It is longer (¾ mile) but the atmosphere is more in keeping with thoughts of the moment. A long pier juts into the water just below the town plaza. From it are better views, past Point Agate opposite, of the Cascades and Mount Rainier.

One wonders how often Chief Seattle enjoyed that view.

Round trip 2 miles
Allow 2 hours
Good all year
Paved road and beach

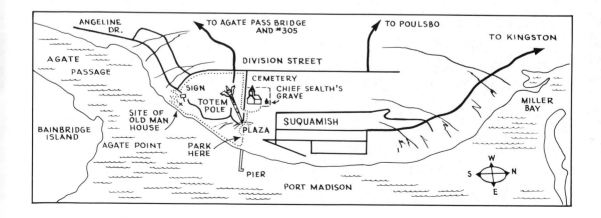

57   POINT NO POINT

Charles Wilkes may have been disappointed when he neared this point of land on his voyage of discovery into Puget Sound in 1841, but for us, Point No Point will go down in our notebooks as a major discovery — a superb beach hike, with an interesting lighthouse for good measure.

The Northern Indians, we are told, coined the name, while the Southern Indians decidedly acknowledged existence of a point by calling it "Long Nose." Whether Wilkes knew this is not certain, but someone in his party jotted in the journal a caustic note that they drew near a point, only to find no point at all; so Wilkes logged it as Point No Point, thus making the name official.

Take cross-Sound ferry to either Winslow or Kingston. From Winslow, drive north on State 305 across Agate Pass Bridge and turn right (east) to Suquamish at end of bridge. At Suquamish, turn left (north) through town and continue 13 miles. (From Kingston ferry landing go west 4 miles to this highway and turn north.) Just before reaching Hansville at the bottom of a long grade, look for a road marked "Point No Point." Turn right past Point No Point Resort, to gate just before lighthouse. During visitors' hours (1 to 3 p.m. weekdays and 1 to 4 p.m. Sundays) park in marked area inside the gate. Other hours, return to the resort, where public parking is available, or walk to the residence and ask the Coast Guard officer. He will be happy to grant permission to park if it is explained your purpose is a hike on the beach.

If the time is right, visit the lighthouse first before hiking. Also take note of the plaque on the lawn, commemorating the signing of an Indian treaty.

Begin the hike on the beach below the parking lot. Across the water to the northwest, look past the town of Hansville to Foulweather Bluff. A light buoy offshore is a test light for Point No Point operators. When it cannot be seen, they start up the fog signal. Straight north, off Double Bluff on Whidbey Island, is another green-and-white signal light. When the green light becomes invisible, Point No Point station activates its fog horn. East across the bluffs of Scatchet Head on the southern tip of Whidbey and beyond Edmonds on the mainland is a magnificent spread of Cascade peaks, stretching south to Mount Rainier.

Walk around the Point (pardon — NO point) below the lighthouse and continue south. Government property extends a mile, to the fringe of woods at the first hill that meets the beach; and all this is yours to walk or dig clams without objection. Pilot Point, jutting to the left, or east of the lighthouse, is 2 more miles on private but as yet undeveloped property; the light station officers say private owners have never objected to hikers, since so far all have been well-behaved. As long as no one breaks the rules regarding litter or beach fires, hikers may continue to use the beach.

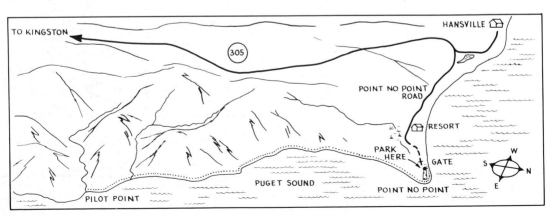

The lighthouse was erected in 1879, and the first signature in the visitors' register was entered in 1895. The original tower still stands. In it, a kerosene lamp was first used, with a steam-operated fog signal. Electric light and diesel compressors have replaced them. The beacon is visible 13 miles out; the fog signal is audible 6 miles.

All this to prove that there is a point to Point No Point.

Round trip 6 miles
Allow 3½ hours
Good anytime
Sand-and-rock beach

Lighthouse on Point No Point

58   BYWATER BAY

There's a little of Robinson Crusoe in us all. Strange that we so seldom get away from our pressures to indulge the Crusoe fantasy. Yet many "escape" valves are tucked away in the innumerable folds of our inland waters. This sandy beach strip is complete with agates, driftwood, a backwater, bird-filled lagoon, and a new experience: walking on water to an island off shore. (Secret: a sandbar about ankle-depth.)

Early in 1968, purchase of 131 acres for future development as a new waterfront state park site was announced. But go now — B.C. (Before Culture.) It is idyllic as is — au naturel.

Take cross-Sound ferry to Winslow, follow highway across Hood Canal Floating Bridge, and turn right at west end of bridge onto Bywater Bay Road. Immediately turn right again, back in the direction of the bridge, on a gravel road that descends steeply to a power station on shore. Park a distance away from the powerhouse and begin hike on the dirt track that cuts across to the shore. A dry lagoon to the left is piled with logs, caught there by extreme high tides.

The state park tidelands reach from the bridge 1½ miles, so hike north along the beach to another larger lagoon. Watch for deer — watching you — from deep woods near the lagoon. Nature trails through these woods are part of state park plans. Agate hunting and clamming are popular, though residents say the beach has been "dug out." Bird-lovers hole up for hours against a driftwood backrest to count and observe the birds around the marshy lagoon.

A little north of the lagoon a spit reaches out to clutch Hood's Head, properly a peninsula, but usually an island. In summer, at extreme low tides, the spit can be crossed easily by wading across the connecting sandspit to Hood's Head — a green-velvet pendant hanging from the necklace of water around the peninsula. Caution: start across only when the tide is going OUT (or you will be marooned on the Head). This gives time to hike another mile to the northeast end of Hood's Head at Point Hannon, for views north across Hood Canal to Foulweather Bluff and southeast to Port Gamble. Summer cottages and some permanent homes line the shores of Hood's Head. Their residents do not wade the reef to reach their homes, but row or chug across channel in boats, leaving cars parked on the mainland road.

If timed properly, the return to the mainland across the underwater sandspit can be made before the tide comes in and buries it too deeply. Swimming back may not be to your liking! If it comes to that, however, there is an escape route. A permanent spit exists to the north which remains above water. To get down a high bluff to it through woods is the hard part. Residents, when trapped, use this outlet. From the north end of the spit they walk a trail that leads to a county road connecting with Bywater Bay Road.

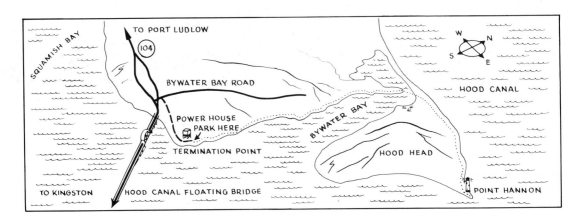

Bywater beach and Hood Canal

Round trip 5 miles
Allow 3½ hours
Good all year
Sand-and-rock beach; check tide table

135

59   PORT TOWNSEND

But for the williwaws of time, Port Townsend might have become the "Key City of the Northwest." There was a period when its sea commerce was second in the nation only to that of New York. It was a city with a thousand bright hopes that flourished, then died. Now, ironically, visitors come to see the only city that has had the foresight to preserve an irreplaceable Victorian charm.

Those who arrive by land are slightly cheated. Only by sailing into port as the pioneers did can one get the full effect of the double-decker "Old Town" look.

If possible, then, plan a Port Townsend visit via auto-ferry from Keystone on Whidbey Island (turn west at Coupeville and follow signs). This is the least-known and most interesting of our Northwest water trips, and gives an excellent gull's-eye view offshore of the city's lower (business district) level, and upper (residential area) level. Drive off ferry dock one block to Water Street, the "main drag," turn right to the far end of the street, and park near a small boat haven.

The route by land, if chosen, is via Hood Canal Floating Bridge north from Kingston (State 104) or Winslow (State 3) or north on US 101. At junction with Port Angeles highway, turn right on State 113. The highway enters Port Townsend on Water Street. Park at far end as above.

Begin the hike with a look at an old Makah Indian canoe — walk around the lower end of the boat basin to the shore. The hand-hewn canoe is on display at almost the point where Captain George Vancouver, exploring in a small boat, realized as the morning fog suddenly lifted that he was entering another bay. He named it for an English marquis.

Return to Water Street at Madison. The old City Hall, built in 1891, now houses the county historical museum and is open to visitors at irregular hours. It is well worth the browsing time. The basement jail once hosted Jack London. Pick up a town map here, or if closed ask for one in a downtown restaurant or store. It will be indispensable for the city tour that follows.

Cruise along Water Street first, noting dates chiseled into still-sturdy portals. The corner hardware store next to the Bartlett Building, built 1881, occupies the rooms of a notorious tavern. Men were given knock-out drops and shanghaied by dropping them from a trap door in the rear to waiting ships. On Adams Street, look hillward. The Leader Building, softened with ivy and the crowsfeet of time, is believed to be the oldest standing all-stone building in the state (1874). Once the territorial courthouse, it now is the town newspaper plant. Walk uphill on Washington

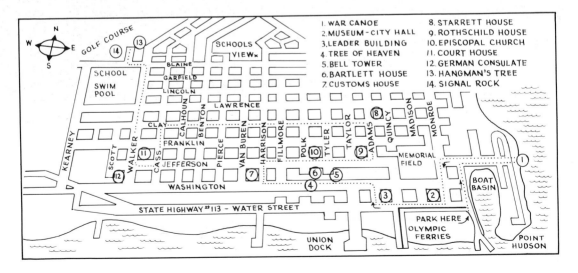

1. WAR CANOE
2. MUSEUM - CITY HALL
3. LEADER BUILDING
4. TREE OF HEAVEN
5. BELL TOWER
6. BARTLETT HOUSE
7. CUSTOMS HOUSE
8. STARRETT HOUSE
9. ROTHSCHILD HOUSE
10. EPISCOPAL CHURCH
11. COURT HOUSE
12. GERMAN CONSULATE
13. HANGMAN'S TREE
14. SIGNAL ROCK

Old German Consulate Building and City Hall at Port Townsend

Street to the town's upper level. Don't miss the Chinese Tree of Heaven, on a slope to the left, near Polk Street. It was a gift from the Emperor of China. Nor the old bell tower on the right, used to signal firemen.

At the top of the hill, turn right (east) to see beautifully preserved old Victorian houses, then walk west for other landmarks. The plan below shows the most interesting.

Round trip 1 to 5 miles
Allow 3 hours at least
Good all year
Paved streets

60   DUNGENESS SPIT

"The low, sandy point of land, which from its great resemblance to Dungeness in the British Channel I called New Dungeness . . ." Captain George Vancouver wrote on his cruise into Juan de Fuca Strait in 1792. He did not know it, but he was naming the longest natural sandspit in the United States.

Dungeness Spit has hardly changed from that day. Praise be!

What can surpass the exhilaration of walking miles on a solitary sandy spit that seems to ride the crest of waves far out into the ocean? It is a rebirth of spirit, swept clean by pounding surf, warm sun, and pungent salt air. Start early and carry a lunch: this driftwood dining room has an endless choice of free-form chairs and tables. Don't be deceived by bright sun: wear a windbreaker jacket over bathing suit or shorts, and roll an extra sweater, scarf, and slacks in the rucksack for chilly breezes of late afternoon. Shoes? Zoris have my vote. The slip-grab pace of a long hike pulls leg muscles but in exchange is the ecstacy of warm sand squishing between toes.

The former public access from Anderson Road now is restricted. While the ban on foot travel to the Spit from here may be lifted later, U.S. Fish and Wildlife Service meanwhile has developed another access trail across the canyon.

Drive US 101 to Sequim. Continue through stop light in town center 4.3 miles. Turn right on Kitchen Road (road name changes later). Continue north 3.4 miles. The road turns right and in .1 mile is Dungeness Recreation Area, a county park. From park entrance bear right then northerly to parking lot at the trail head. The footpath winds through a timber stand, crosses an open area once used as sheep pasture, jogs east, then north where it connects with an old trail from the bluff which ends at the "throat" of the Spit.

This 7-mile-long tongue of land has 20 miles of beach and is surprisingly diverse, not monotonous. A 10-foot wall of driftwood is piled in the center — so high one cannot see over it. Outside, facing the Strait, only the screech of gulls is heard over waves that pound the shore into smooth, hard-packed sand. Seashells, bark slabs, great wheels of sliced logs, and anything from tiny chips to huge crates with Japanese lettering can be seen.

Inside, facing the mainland, is the softer face, patted by the ripples of a saltwater lagoon formed by Graveyard Spit on the east. The sand

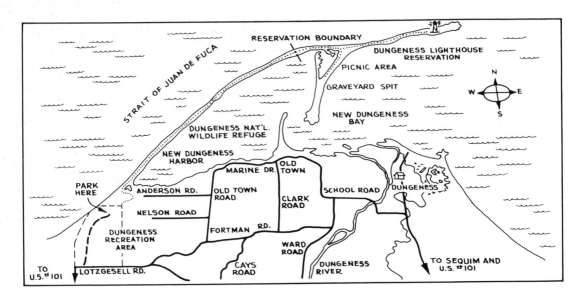

is soft and caressing; birds pip and squeak and squeal and shriek over and around the hiker. Crossing over the thick driftwood wall is not always easy, except where the jeep track made by lighthouse personnel is seen.

This 556 acres of sand, tideland, and saltwater is protected as Dungeness National Wildlife Refuge and is closed from October 1 to March 1 to provide a feeding and resting area for thousands of black brant and ducks of all kinds during migrations and in winter. More thousands of shore birds also frequent the area. Though bird populations are lower in summer, they are always around in numbers for bird-lovers to identify or simply enjoy. Harbor seals also are seen loafing on shore. Larger groups congregate in fall.

The hike to the lighthouse at the end makes a full day. If time is limited, turn back about halfway, where Graveyard Spit breaks off and reaches for the mainland. A picnic area is maintained there. (No overnight camping permitted.) Graveyard Spit got its name, the story goes, from the days of the British-American boundary dispute. A party of Canadian Indians, who often made trips across the Strait to trade goods with American settlers, supposedly were robbed and murdered by rivals and their bodies were buried on the lonely sandspit.

Clam digging is excellent at low tide. Butter, little neck, horseneck, and cockles are easily obtained; at extreme low tides, some geoducks may be taken.

So Captain Vancouver gave it a nod and a name as he passed by. How could he know what he was missing?

Round trip 14 miles
Allow 6 hours
Good March 1-September 30
Dirt road, sandy beach

Dungeness Spit

61   BLAKE ISLAND

By its very isolation and relatively-unchanged appearance, Blake Island is invested with an exotic air. So near a 1969 city, yet still a pre-pioneer setting. More, it offers a unique Northwest experience. Where else can one walk completely around an island? This singularly beautiful hike can be done along a rough dirt road that circles the isle or on the beach below. Or combine them, diverging easily from one to the other.

Blake's isolation also is a drawback, unless one has a boat. (There are moorage floats for boaters, and after the busy summer tour season, more room at the 300-foot pier at Tillicum Village on the northeast point of the island.) No beach fires are permitted, but there are overnight campsites.

For non-boatowners, Tillicum Village tours are the answer. From June to Labor Day cruisers leave Harbor Tours Dock, Pier 56 on Seattle's waterfront. The normal tour is too short to allow time for the 2-hour hike, but special arrangements can be made for return when calling for reservations, EA 2-6444. Verify the return on a later boat than the tour party when the ticket is purchased, and again at the Village artifacts counter before starting the hike. Tour price, $8.00 for adults and $5.00 for children under 12, includes a delicious barbecued salmon dinner

cooked in the traditional Makah Indian style and entertainment of interpretive Northwest Indian songs and dances.

Begin the hike on the road behind the restaurant building. Go left, past park ranger's trailers. For the beach walk, continue straight to the shore. For the land walk, follow the road as it swings right into woods shortly before the beach, and keep bearing left wherever forks appear. The beach route has only one difficult rocky shelf, at Madrona Point on the southeast end. Two picnic sites with tables are on the beach about a mile apart. At these points the road comes close by, allowing a switch in routes.

The road walk is a botanist's delight. The island's former owner-residents, the William Pitt Trimbles, imported many rare trees which have survived to mingle with indigenous species. One enters a succession of varied groves as the road dips up and down like a mild rollercoaster, out of sunlight and into shade of alder, cedar, Douglas fir, hemlock, yew, beech, cottonwood, cascara, laurel, and magnificent maples mantled in ivy. And always, on shore edge, the Northwest's beach emblem, the lovely madrona. From bluff points, between the trees, catch views of Vashon Island, Southworth ferry dock, the Space Needle, Magnolia Bluff, Bainbridge Island, West Seattle. Civilization seems far away. Feel curious eyes on you? One of four dozen deer on the island.

Blake was circled by Captain Vancouver in 1792 but was not named until the Wilkes expedi-

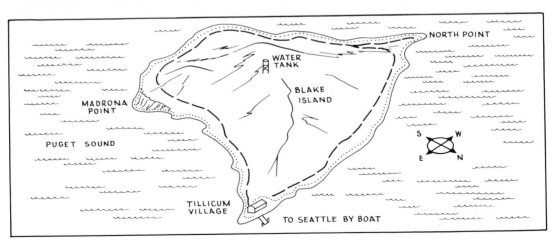

Indian long house at Tillicum Village

tion in 1841. The Trimbles purchased the island about 1908, built an estate, and left when their home burned. The foundation can be seen about 200 yards beyond the first turn in the trail. William Hewitt's Tillicum Village and 4½ acres of the marine park's 475 acres are leased from the state.

Round trip by beach 6½ miles, by road 4 miles
Allow 2 hours by road, 3½ by beach
Best in summer, but good anytime
Easy dirt road or rock-and-sand beach

141

62   DOLPHIN POINT

No one who has lived on Vashon Island ever wants to leave. Until that event most islanders dread — the coming of a bridge allowing quick-and-easy passage from the mainland — the ferry drops the visitor into instant tranquillity and oddly-detached, pastoral beauty.

Drive, or take the No. 18 Lincoln Park bus, to Fauntleroy Ferry dock in West Seattle (call Washington State Ferries for schedules) and ride the waves 3 miles to Vashon. Without a car, one can do the north-end hike around Dolphin Point and return to take the ferry home, or catch a bus from the ferry dock to Burton for the woods hike on Burton Peninsula (Hike 64).

Walk the main highway uphill to the left a short distance from the ferry dock. A trail begins at a group of mailboxes on the left side of the road. Follow it about ½ mile, skirting the bluff above beach houses, then climb a set of log-banked steps to reach an upper trail.

Continue east on the upper path. In about 200 yards the wide lane narrows and is a bit overgrown. The views from this bluff 50 feet above beach cottages, perched on individual bulkheads, looking over the Sound toward West Seattle or past the ferry dock to Bainbridge Island, are as lovely now as when this writer traipsed along the trail to visit neighbors, or dashed to catch the ferry for work at Boeing

during the war. About ¼ mile along is "Grandpappy," my favorite tree, an enormous Douglas fir 6 feet through. Several more of his aged family are scattered in woods to the right. In spring tiny, fragile starflower carpets the bank, and trilliums and forget-me-nots wink from among the ferns. A few hundred feet beyond Grandpappy a gravel road meets the trail and broadens into a parking lot.

In the 1940s, when Betty McDonald of **Egg and I** fame lived here, most islanders with homes beyond the point hiked the entire trail to the ferry. Since the road was built this section has been neglected. The road continues around Dolphin Point and heads south, high above unbelievable beach homes with spacious, green lawns, well-tended plantings and orchards, and front yards piled high with bleached driftwood. A large, brown house about ¼ mile from the point was home for Betty McDonald, and the focal point of her book, **Onions in the Stew.** The road ends at a private house about ½ mile from the parking area but a narrow trail continues. It ascends slightly, then dips to end, seemingly, in an overgrown tangle of berry vines. End the hike here and return as you came, or if you wish a longer, varied route, pick a way carefully over two or three wooden planks for the next few yards, sighting for a large wooden trestle or platform ahead. From the trestle, a road leads uphill among big trees, climbing steeply to come out on a lane between barn and buildings of two farmhouses. Talk conversationally to the barking dogs as they

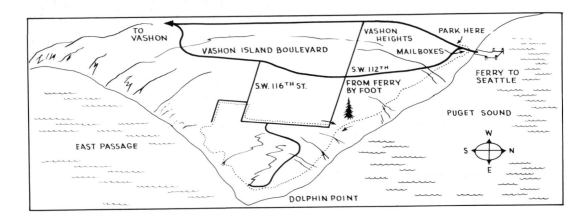

Dolphin Point and ferry dock

bound out to interrogate. Continue 1/2 block to S.W. 116th Street. Turn left to the highway if you wish to follow the pavement down to the ferry dock. Or to return to the trail, continue straight through the intersection to S. W. 112th Street, which deadends here, together with your street. Find the trail at the end of a dirt driveway which drops swiftly downhill between ivy-covered banks under tall alders. Turn left on the trail it meets to continue to the ferry dock.

Round trip 2 1/2 miles
Allow 1 1/2 hours
Good all year
Trail and road

63   ROBINSON POINT

Feel like escaping somewhere for a little while, where you can fling your arms wide and walk for miles beside the sea? To talk to no one but seagulls and brush the cobwebs out of your brain?

One need not drive a hundred miles. Not more than 3 miles out in Puget Sound is an ideal place for a picnic lunch and hike on the beach with the bonus of a visit to one of our few remaining Coast Guard light stations.

Follow directions for ferry to Vashon Island (see Hike 62) and drive on the main road from the dock through the town of Vashon. Continue south on 99th Avenue S.W. to 204th Street and turn left (east) at Vashon High School. Follow to unmarked junction — either road goes to Portage. Left is a nice beach drive which rejoins the other at a fork just beyond KIRO transmitter station. Take the left. (To right is Docton.) A later sign,

Lighthouse on Robinson Point

144

beyond KING Radio tower, says "Robinson Road," which meets S.W. 240th about 1.4 miles farther. Continue east on 240th about 1.3 miles to an unmarked fork. Turn right (south) on road which leads to the light station on the beach. Ample parking is provided.

The light station is open to visitors weekdays from 1 to 3 p.m. and on weekends and holidays 1 to 4 p.m. (Not always open in winter.) Be sure to include a visit if open. The beach south may be open only in the afternoon.

There are miles of beach — mostly rocks, some sand — that stretch on both sides of the point. A good day's stroll is 4 miles, heading north, then west, to Portage. Southward a similar distance one reaches the site of old gravel pits. In any weather the stroll is invigorating. On crisp, clear days, splendid views are added — Mount Rainier looms in the southwest, and one almost seems able to reach across to touch Three Tree Point, jutting into East Passage on the north. Endless piles of driftwood in interesting shapes draw the collector, especially south of the point. Curl up out of the wind behind a bleached stump to partake of that picnic lunch.

Cobwebs have no chance in that setting!

Robinson Point is the extreme eastern tip of Maury Island, which dangles off Vashon proper by a toothpick isthmus that looks, on the map, as though it might break off at any moment. Maury looks free-floating and almost separate, but the map makes it obvious it fitted snugly at one time to the mother island. Even Burton Peninsula looks like a lost tooth that once fitted into Maury's jaw. Because Robinson Point juts into the East Passage shipping route to Tacoma and Olympia, it has had a light station since 1893.

The first light to mark the point for early captains was a lantern on a wooden arm. A more solid wooden, open-frame tower was built about 1894 to house the old lens lantern. The present light tower which replaced the structure in 1915 housed a stronger lens. The lens and frame currently in use were made in Paris about 50 years ago. A 500-watt bulb shining in the tower 40 feet above the water is visible 15 miles, but when fog sets in another signal goes into action. The early system was a 12-inch steam whistle; later, reed-type trumpet horns were installed (the holes for them are still visible in the tower) and now improved horns sound a 4-second blast every 20 seconds during foggy periods.

The very first entry in the visitors' log was made by a Mrs. C. M. Sherman on February 5, 1893. Some 21,056 visitors signed the log after her, including yours truly. By the time you add yours, a few thousand more will have been added.

Round trip your choice: 1 to 8 miles
Allow a half or full day
Good anytime
Easy beach but rocky

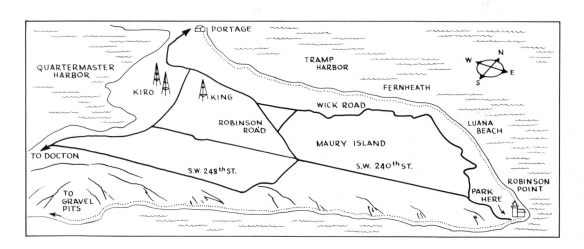

64   BURTON PENINSULA

Burton, near the southern end of Vashon Island, is a "name town" — the citizens claim it for a mailing address but live scattered about on surrounding beaches and countryside. But the town has its memories of near-greatness. It was named in 1892 for a town in Illinois, and that year Vashon College, a co-educational preparatory school, was founded. In the same decade ocean-going transports and an occasional four-master made busy traffic into the fine inland Quartermaster Harbor, and waited their turns for repairs at a busy drydock in Docton across the bay.

The college is long-since gone, destroyed by fire in 1912 and never rebuilt. The big ships are ghosts on a quiet harbor filled only with small pleasure craft; Burtonites prefer it that way.

Follow directions for ferry to Vashon (see Hike 62) and take bus or drive from ferry dock on main road (Vashon Island Blvd.) through the island's main town, Vashon, south to Burton.

Part of this hike is an old favorite of Campfire Girls, through a patch of deep woods hidden from outsiders looking in. Go east from Burton on 240th Street .3 mile to Bayview Road. Park here on shoulder and begin hike going right on the paved road. Bayview makes a complete circle of Burton Peninsula and our destination is almost midway. At .7 mile is Jensen's Point, with a county public boat launch site and small picnic area. Walk north on road to the second house, where a high stump is centered in a grassy plot near the road. Just opposite this stump, look sharp into the brush. A low stump just past the brush marks the beginning of a trail. Once past the brushy camouflage, the trail is wide and distinct.

One steps into an outdoor living room hung with verdant draperies. The ceiling arches in solid green to seal out the world, so close, yet so far behind. A pavement of needles silences the footsteps, so birds in their haven are not disturbed. The path winds uphill past huge stumps above a small ravine, so thickly grown over one hardly can trace its outline. Berry vines and salal crowd the floor, dotted with wildflowers and huge mushrooms. Side-trails are numerous; to mark the main path for the return might be wise, but one hardly can get lost in this circular forest emerald: work outward from any point to arrive at the circumference road.

About 1/3 mile, the path comes to a Campfire Girl Council Ring, with rustic benches forming an outdoor theater. Stop here; a few feet beyond, the trail ends at several buildings and a high water tank. These are camp buildings used annually by Baptists for summer youth assemblies. Do not trespass on this private property, but return to Jensen's Point. Finish the circle on Bayview Road back to the car.

Linger on the side-paths as you will, with thoughts, we trust, of appreciation to islanders for preserving this tiny forest nugget.

Round trip 1½ miles
Allow 1 hour
Good anytime
Easy trail

Stump along Burton Peninsula path

65   LOWER GREEN RIVER

For many persons the only approach to the Green River is at the private lodge and resort 4 miles east of Black Diamond. But this "ribbon of wilderness . . . a corridor of natural history with open shelves of geological displays for man to explore," as naturalist Wolf Bauer describes it, offers rare scenic splendor. Water has many sounds: the crashing crescendo of a waterfall; the fortissimo of ocean breakers. But a river has happy musical tones — an adagio of lazy pools, a deep, purposeful andante flow, a capriccioso as the current slaps a sandbar, piles itself into a frenzied scherzo and recovers, sliding in a pianissimo sedately to sea.

A good way to learn to know a river (and fall under its spell) is to work upstream. This first of four hikes begins east of Auburn.

Drive Interstate 5 south and take Auburn exit east to the off-ramp marked "Black Diamond-Green River Valley" 2 miles past Auburn. Turn right on Black Diamond Road. In less than .1 mile, bear right at fork to Green River Valley Road and park on wide shoulder by river. Follow a trail going downstream under three bridges— freeway, railroad and concrete. It mounts a 10-foot overgrown bank (muddy in spring, crusty in fall), winds around railroad bridge supports, and in ¼ mile become a wide, level gravel path edging the river.

In fall, the river's happy, impish mood is shared by fishermen who line its banks and wade its ripples midstream. The camaraderie of these outdoorsmen makes November and December, when the air is crisp and clear, as enjoyable a time for this hike as any — perhaps better than most. Across the river, by the railroad bridge, where the wide mouth of Soos Creek spills its waters into the river, the wilderness still seems to remain, despite the clatter and whoosh of traffic across the freeway and iron bridge nearby. From behind the hill above the creek the incomparable wail of a train whistle drifts across, then, shrilling imperiously, the locomotive bursts out of the green and rattles onto the bridge. Far back from the river path, farmhouses screened by huge cottonwoods hopefully keep the river at a safe distance in flood season.

Patient, enduring anglers wade deep in the river's gurgling ripples as it splits around a sandbar and charges through a narrow channel. Thin, fragrant plumes of wood smoke from tiny fires stoked by chilled fishermen add a primeval touch. Now and then a triumphant shout pierces the air; a large steelhead is plucked from the swirling water amid envious gazes and congratulations of companions. Infrequently, too, large, dead salmon, spent in spawning up river, are seen drifting at river's edge.

At about ½ mile, the trail rounds the end of a fence, swings left, skirts a brackish pond and loses itself among thickets and young trees as it

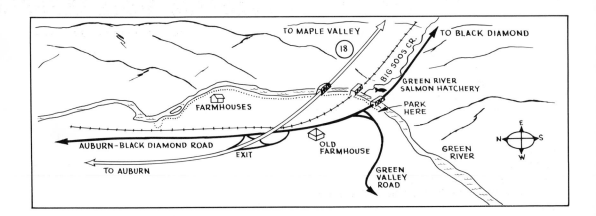

Steelhead fishing in Green River

comes out on the river bank again. Now tamed, the stream ambles docilely beside the railroad right-of-way, civilization's barrier and the end of the hike.

Round trip 1-1/3 miles
Allow 1½ hours
Good anytime except flood season
Short muddy stretch (100 yards) then wide gravel
   path

66   FLAMING GEYSER PARK

Follow directions of Hike 65 to the junction, but proceed past parking area mentioned on fork to the right of iron bridge. This is the lovely Green Valley Road that winds through valley farms, lined in part with maples, over a bridge, and past more farms with many Japanese names on mailboxes. About 7 miles beyond the junction the road ascends briefly, passes a large sand-and-gravel works, and forks halfway up the hill. The left fork continues uphill to Kummer. Take the right over a slight rise, a branch road to Flaming Geyser Park, which dips down to another bridge over the Green and in a little more than a mile comes to the park entrance. The State purchased the former private resort for a park recently and the area is posted pending future development, but park where permitted near the entrance, and walk along the river.

Cross Cristy Creek at the east end of the resort area and hike uphill on a jeep road that winds behind a concrete building. The road soon drops to river level, skirting through deep quiet woods. Unbelievable moss and ferns, sprouting from the vertical green life-line 50 feet up the trunks of towering maples, wave their fronds. In summer, tall berry bushes and Canadian thistle border the path. At about ¾ mile, the rough track ends abruptly at a dry stream bed, which the river seldom seeks except in flood time. Turn right and walk its rocky floor. In a few hundred yards the dry bed opens on a rocky shelf by the river, now charged with chattering rapids. Pick a way on the rocky shore for 100 yards or so to a large boulder. Climb to the top for impressive views upstream. A steep, rocky promontory just beyond juts far out into the river. Unless the water is very low, currently the hike must end here. However, trails will soon be built to continue the hike upriver, along the new easement strip purchased by the Game Department.

Here is the real beginning of the Green River Gorge. Before you are sheer rock cliffs with some of the "open shelves of geological displays" described by Wolf Bauer. Farther upstream can be seen tilted strata with imbedded fossils and sea-life imprints laid down millions of years ago, part of this natural museum. Opposite the rocky promontory that blocks your path is a small, intriguing cave. Here is an amazing world, removed from turmoil, on this stony shelf of a river that has taken countless human lifetimes to cut its rocky channel.

Behind the geyser pool east of the buildings at the start of the hike from the park another trail is marked "Fire Geyser, Sulphur Spring and Cristy Creek." It climbs 10 or 15 feet, drops to cross the creek, follows a small, moss-covered canyon, and continues over a chattering group of freshets that dump into the creek before trailing into woods about a mile.

The name Flaming Geyser came from "geysers" (now inactive) discovered when prospectors drilled holes in search of coal. Gas forced its way through water at irregular intervals and burned brightly when ignited, sometimes for hours. With great ballyhoo the park was developed early in the 1920s by Eastern promoters as a resort to rival Banff, but funds and litigation slowed the development.

Round trip 1½ miles
Allow 1½ hours
Good all year
Dirt track

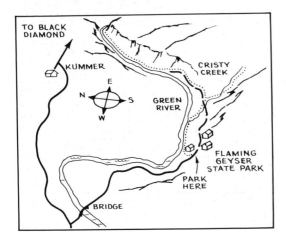

Green River Gorge near Flaming Geyser

67   BLACK DIAMOND BRIDGE

Fishermen have worn many a track to their favorite haunts on Green River banks. One need not bear rod and reel, however, to enjoy their choice views. Some of their trails are difficult — like the steep, muddy trail beginning at the north end of the bridge spanning the river on the Black Diamond-Enumclaw highway. With far less effort, a lesser-known and almost hidden approach from the opposite side leads to an equally rewarding, even more beautiful viewpoint.

Drive 2½ miles south from Black Diamond on State 169 to the Green River Bridge. Cross the bridge and keep a sharp eye open for an un-

Green River Gorge

marked, narrow dirt road on the right (west) ½ mile from the south end of the bridge. Turn in and drive through close growth to a locked gate at a fork .3 mile. The road beyond the gate is a private approach to a target range. Park if there is room, but **DO NOT** block the road for owners entering or leaving. Hikers and fishermen are permitted to use the road as access to the river, but **DO NOT** cross the fence into the target range at any time. It can be extremely dangerous during target practice. Turn right a few yards before the fence on a trail that leads past an outdoor toilet and links up in less than ¼ mile with a road that winds down toward the river.

Ignore side-trails and continue downhill on the main dirt road, which twists through willows and cottonwoods, turns sharp left to a wide bluff high over the river, then narrows to rocky ruts and descends sharply in just under a mile to river level.

In summer, the welcome cover of thickets, alder, and willows laced with berry bushes, the gurgle of the river, act like a cooling sunburn lotion. The road ends in an indistinct trail disappearing through brush, just beyond a ring of blackened campfire stones. Before the campfire is a path to the right which leads into several trails that come to the river's edge in a few hundred yards.

From here, one can — except in high water — hop-scotch or wade among rocks and wide, sandy bars a mile or more upriver and under the bridge. A huge boulder at the edge of perky rapids is a centerpiece in the peaceful scene.

The sheer cliff on the opposite side, topped with firs, is a backdrop for the gorge. An intriguing little cavern at its foot tempts one — it might be reached if the river is very low.

The worst part of this hike is leaving the river, especially on a warm sunny day.

Round trip 1 mile
Allow 1 hour
Good all year
Dirt road

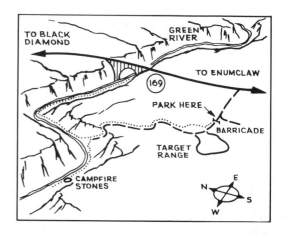

Yellow violet

Sword fern

68   GREEN RIVER GORGE

Stand on the high bridge spanning one of the deepest parts of the Green River Gorge for an instant view of prehistoric eras; down, down, more than 200 feet the eyes cleave across centuries of time, tracing a waterfall that plunges out of the fern-covered cliff south of the bridge, drops into a pool halfway down, breaks into a series of terraces, and finally reaches the river. Far down in the rugged canyon youngsters move from deep, cool shadows into shafts of sun that glint on their hair as they wade over rocks and into eddies behind boulders. Join them! An easy walk, for young and old alike, and the best part of this popular and best-known approach to the Green River Gorge.

Drive State Highway 169 south from Renton to Black Diamond. A large sign in town center marks the road to the Green River Gorge, 4 miles east. Cross the bridge to the east end and park beside the lodge. Cars are not permitted to stop on the bridge.

The privately-owned lodge and resort cabins of red-painted clapboard show their 45 years of age but add a picturesque note to the scene. Sustenance is available from a snack bar and restaurant; a large, grassy picnic grounds across the road from the lodge offers, for a nominal charge, tables and outdoor firepits under huge shade trees. A waterwheel in the creek gives the final, old-world touch.

The rule that cars may not stop on the bridge is a good one, allowing room for strollers to enjoy the view, which takes more than a few moments. (Only a few persons join my small clique who cannot look below without hanging on to the railing for dear life, but we are a special breed.)

The bridge was built in 1914 and has borne many a gasping sightseer since. The fascination of this high outlook changes from month to month as the river rises and falls with the seasons. Looking north, a fair-sized island in the middle of the river seems small from this height, but the tall hemlocks and firs bordering the river banks suggest the true size. The river looks peaceful, approaching from the north, but begins to churn as it is compressed into the chan-

nel passing under the bridge, and splashes and foams in a sudden "frug" twist scooping out an ever-widening curve as it races into the west.

The trail down begins at the side of the lodge (a small charge is made at the gate by resort owners) and is steadied with catwalks to ease the rougher drops, especially one immediately next the waterfall. One drops from beds of salal and wild currant into an engraved volume of natural history, where time and the river have etched out special wading pools. And nothing can equal that sweet smell of damp moss and ferns and pools; the shafts of sunlight stabbing into the canyon and highlighting the ripples; the protective feeling of huge boulders and the fun of clambering over clefts in the shore. It is less than ¼ mile down to the river and in spring the water is too high to go much farther. But in late summer and fall one can hike a mile downstream along the bank. The way is rough, around boulders and over slippery banks in places, but local youngsters have a favorite swimming pool out of sight of the bridge a mile down.

The pool belongs to youth. But Green River belongs to the ages.

Round trip ½ to 2 miles
Allow 1-2 hours
Best July-Oct. May be closed in winter
Dirt path

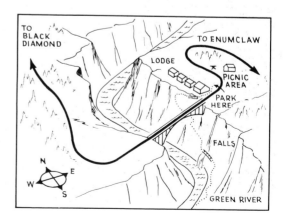

69 DEEP LAKE— NOLTE STATE PARK

A bit of aquamarine buried in woods, adjacent to a highway yet hidden from passing drivers. All the better for the lake to nourish wildflowers and marsh growth in abundance, cuddle birds and small creatures under tall trees, and be cherished by beneficiaries of the original homesteader.

Since first publication of Footloose, the owner of this homestead area, Minnie Nolte, died and left the property to the State Parks and Recreation Commission in her will, because she "wanted the public to have some good" out of it. A beautiful gesture for you and yours; and appropriately the new state park is named for her.

Until the area is renovated and set up for steady public use, depending on fund allocations, there will be changes and work in progress. Meantime, the trail around the lake will be preserved, at latest report, and is available to hikers, but consideration of park employees is expected. Help them preserve the trail — no messing!

Drive State 169 south from Renton to Black Diamond, turn east on Green River Gorge road to Cumberland, then south 1 mile. A sign, "Nolte State Park" on the right marks the entrance. (Another entrance on the west is contemplated for the future.) Picnic tables and facilities on the lake shore, removed for construction, may be restored by the time you visit, but swimming facilities may take longer.

Begin the hike on the road that circles the lake. Either direction — but if you hate making decisions go right from the gate. The road narrows to a wide, needled path after passing some rental cottages, briefly goes deep into woods out of sight of the lake, then returns shoreward among big Douglas firs straddled by vines, waist-high sword fern, and Oregon grape. Cedars drape lacy boughs over the path.

Near the north end, about ¾ mile, where a tiny brook runs into the lake, watch quietly from among gnarled trees, musky yarrow, and devil's club while birds, startled from their stakeouts in a pile of snags and logs, gather confidence and return to their perches. A slight ascent leads to the big-tree area west of the lake. Some are 6 feet in diameter. A few bear lightning scars. Under the trees are more picnic tables, tucked in private niches by the shore.

The lake probably was named early in the homesteading era, when it was believed to reach a depth of 400 feet. The official maximum depth is now given as 76 feet, still far from a wading pool.

Miss Nolte's father owned a part of the property since 1883, and the remainder was granted to him by President Benjamin Harrison in 1889. Her brother began operating the resort around the 39-acre, Deep Lake about 1913, and a concessionaire operated it from 1928 until her death. The 117-acre area was logged in the long-ago when only easy-to-take trees were cut; this accounts for those lovely big trees. One rule steadfastly upheld at the resort in the past was: No motorboats. No noise. It was a favorite of many families for years. In memory of Miss Nolte and her thoughtful legacy to us, let's hope the peace and beauty of her lake and grove endure.

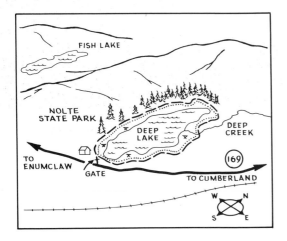

Round trip 1½ miles
Allow 1 hour
Good all year
Wide path

Woods Trail, Deep Lake

70   McDONALD POINT LOOKOUT

Look not longingly on the Cascade peaks and assume they are much too far for you to enjoy. Only an hour's drive from Seattle are lookout stations — not the topmost peaks, admittedly, thrilling views. McDonald Point Lookout is one of these.

Drive State Highway 169 about 3 miles south of Maple Valley and turn left (east) at sign for Ravensdale (S.E. 272nd Street). In 2 miles, just past Ravensdale County Park, cross Hobart Road and continue 1 mile to a fork. Take right branch marked Kanasket and go past a Baptist Bible Camp 3 miles to Kanasket Junction where a bridge spans the railroad. Do not cross the bridge but swing sharp left along the railroad as it turns north. At .7 mile, park well off the road near driveway marked "SE Courtney Road." Take picnic lunch and water, as the hike is long and steep. (Fill canteens from a cascade a mile above.) Hike up driveway past houses, over railroad tracks and immediately turn left. A large, yellow gate blocks vehicles here, except those for logging work.

Under no circumstances attempt to drive ANY vehicle into the driveway. You cross private property to reach the logging road and gate. The owner welcomes true hikers but after tormenting summers of roar and dust of traffic (especially motorcycles with beastly mannered drivers!) now prohibits all private vehicles. WALK in—with good manners and nothing noisier than a smile.

The climb is gradual but steady; the way is pleasant and cool through second-growth forest, shading ferns and wildflowers. An abandoned gravel pit with broken shoring appears and in ¾ mile more is a wide fork. Property below the fork is Weyerhaeuser Company land; above is Northern Pacific Railway's. Access is by their permission—accept with courtesy and care.

The left branch, a deadend, disappears in the greenery downhill. Follow the right branch — the steepest part of the hike—to the former lookout in just short of 1 more mile. Each step brings more views over green valleys to the northeast as far as Mount Baker. Approaching the broad, open, sundrenched knob the hiker is unprepared for a delicious shock. A chill breeze seems to blow over his shoulder. He turns — and gasps. Mount Rainier is so close he almost ducks instinctively!

A fine panorama sweeping from Rainier, over the Green River snaking through green forests, and west over nearby Sugarloaf Mountain, Lake Retreat and Lake Walsh, far through the blue haze to the Olympics, finally north to Baker and other Cascade peaks.

The mountain was named for Robert McDonald, a timber cruiser, field inspector, and fire warden for the Washington Forest Fire Association.

Round trip 7½ miles
Allow 5 hours
High point 3280 feet
Elevation gain 2300 feet
Best March to November, often good in winter
Dirt road

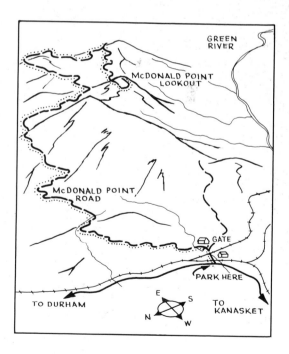

Mount Rainier and top of McDonald Point

71   MOUNT PETE

A short but steep hike, Mt. Pete (also known as Mount Peak or Pinnacle Peak) is a favorite with families for its easy accessibility and its intimate tone — a view from an outdoor studio.

Drive east from Enumclaw on US 410 and turn right at 284th Ave. S.E. to S.E. 472nd St. Turn right (west), curving with the road ½ mile along Mt. Pete's north side. Park beside the road where it makes a sharp right turn north. The unmarked trail begins just at the corner of the turn, taking off steeply through sword fern, berries, bracken, and salal under maples and second-growth firs.

The trail switchbacks often. Frogs croak under moss-covered limbs "all gang aglay." Cedars and Douglas firs grow ever bigger next to old stumps; at a bend in the trail, wet banks are upholstered with delicate fronds of maidenhair fern. Devil's club spreads huge leaves. Vine maple splashes the tucks and folds of the hill with flame red in fall. Bare clay, slippery when wet, and many exposed roots require caution in places.

About ½ mile (it seems twice that) the trail levels to meet a gravel service road. Continue uphill on the road, past a turnaround, to a sharp right turn. At the turn are fascinating forma-tions of columnar basalt. Man's efforts at building seem puny beside these rocks that appear to have been chiseled, planed, and stacked side by side like a stone logpile. The road now climbs steeply and swings left to a level terrace below the boulder-strewn, knobby summit.

The lookout tower of former years is gone but from atop the boulders are splendid views. Mt. Rainier dominates the scene south; west are Puget Sound and the Olympics. Northeast, beyond Baldy Hill, is gloomy-looking Mt. Enumclaw, "place of the evil spirits," named, according to legend, by Indians who camped one night at its base and fled in fright during a terrible thunderstorm. The town of Enumclaw, on a plain between the White and Green Rivers, was named for the mountain when it was platted in 1885. Settlers came slowly at first. A small rowboat, used as a ferry across White River, was summoned by blowing a cow's horn hidden in a stump. Then came the railroad and loggers — and cash money in place of the skins and hides previously used in trading. Now the valley, seen from the mountain, looks like a quiet jigsaw puzzle of farms, barns, and pastures.

A longer but easier route to the summit is from the south side. Turn south from US 410 in Enumclaw on 268th St. S.E., which jogs right, then left, to an intersection with Mud Mountain Road, 1.7 miles. Turn left to a small parking area in less than ½ mile, opposite entrance to gated service road on the left. Park and walk up the road, ascending through alder and fir groves. At a junction in ½ mile, take the right fork to top.

One wonders: what became of the cow's horn? Is it still hidden in a stump, these 80 long years?

Round trip 2 miles (north side);
  3 miles (south side)
Allow 2½ hours
High point 1801 feet
Elevation gain 1100 feet
Good all year
Trail and dirt road

Columnar basalt near summit of Mount Pete

72 MOUNT PHILIP

Have your small fry learned the meaning of "dappled sunlight?" Or seen skunk cabbage in a cool, forest swamp? Do you have trouble explaining what it was like when pioneers pushed wagon trains through deep woods to get Way Out West — to Puget Sound?

Take them up Mt. Philip — a perfect afternoon hike that gives the feel of an explorer's trail and bursts out of forest on a tiny platform atop the hill, with a splendid view of the White River snaking its way far below.

Drive south on Interstate 5 to exit for Enumclaw (State 410) east. Seven miles from Enumclaw on State 410 turn right on side road (sign "Mt. Philip Trail" may be gone) that ascends briefly and parallels the highway for a mile before it rejoins the pavement. Midway is a small turnout with a picnic table and room for two or three cars. Park here, or if you can't squeeze in, go on to the highway, park, and walk back. A few paces beyond the picnic table is the start of the trail. A tiny sign reads: "Vista Point Trail ½ mile."

The trail descends and skirts a boggy marsh, brightened in spring with yellow-and-green skunk cabbage. Despite the tangle of growth the trail is well-kept, though twig-strewn and muddy in spots; where difficult, steps are hewn out of logs and over one bog lies a long plank bridge.

Now a slow ascent under tall trees with huge fern "boots." The sun disappears. A startled chipmunk runs over a moss-covered log. The trail switchbacks, ever steeper. There is the sweet, dank smell of a forest grown around and over 5-foot stumps and massive, spreading roots of older giants. Today's trees are not large, but are so numerous the trail is dark even on a sunny day — a fine example of a forest that thins itself as stronger trees dominate.

Only one trail fork is troublesome: In ½ mile, a post shows simply an arrow pointing right into brush. Trust the arrow. Puff a little up the switchbacks; the twittering forest noises cease, all is silent. Suddenly, burst out of woods onto a tiny pinnacle. The sweeping panorama is briefly dizzying, but a flat boulder provides a seat for steadier viewing.

To the east are Cascade foothills and peaks. From your vantage point almost at the top of Mt. Philip, the view extends far to the north. Unfortunately the pinnacle rock hides Rainier to the south. At the tips of your toes, 500 feet below, the White River snuggles lazily around a wide sandbar on its way from Greenwater, Naches Pass, and Rainier.

Mt. Philip was named by a Weyerhaeuser Company forester for John Philip Weyerhaeuser, Jr., then president of the company, who died of leukemia in the early 1950s. The area was logged in 1931 and the present forest grew rapidly around the old stumps. The trail was put in by the company for the enjoyment of the public.

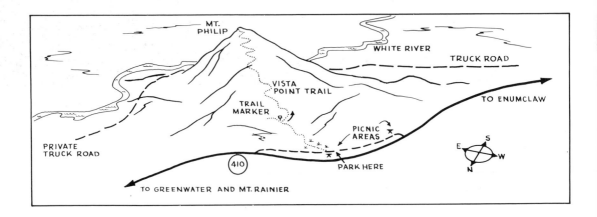

White River from Mount Philip

Round trip 1 mile
Allow 1 hour
High point 1700 feet
Elevation gain 310 feet
Best March to October, good much of the winter
Dirt trail

163

73 FEDERATION FOREST STATE PARK

Every hiker must begin somewhere. Since the earliest hikers were pioneers, why not start with them?

Of Washington State's historical highlights, none is more dramatic or thrilling than the saga of the first wagon train to come over the Naches Pass. After the Longmire party in 1853 lowered their wagons down a steep cliff with ropes made of cattle hides, rather than turn back, they left a trace of their anxious finale in what is now Federation Forest State Park. Now, thanks to a group of women endowed with great foresight, we, too, can play pioneer and see the land exactly as the earliest arrivals did.

Drive approximately 17 miles east from Enumclaw on Chinook Pass Highway, US 410. Parking lot is by the Interpretive Center. View the exhibits first before hiking. Living displays outside the Center and explanatory pictorial panels illustrate the widely-diverse beauty and character of flora in the seven biotic zones found in this state.

The Forest is open every day, all year; but the Interpretive Center only April 1 through September 30 (plus a few winter weekends and holidays).

Group nature tours will be conducted by the ranger on duty by prearrangement (call Enumclaw 663-2207). Otherwise a leaflet with map can be picked up at the desk, sufficient to guide one on the nature trails — a short, "East" trail of $\frac{3}{8}$ mile and a longer "West" trail of .9 mile. Extensions on the Naches and Maltby trails add another $\frac{1}{4}$ mile. For further comprehension and enjoyment a larger trail guidebook is sold ($1.00). Couched in simple terms with drawings, it helps explain features seen or marked on the trail — changing ecosystems, a tree healing a wound or struggling for a century to keep from falling over, even a dead snag which offers haven for birds and insects, all calculated to add a third eye for future jaunts. The "Land of the Giants" is guaranteed to draw gasps and stretch your necks.

Traces of the pioneers? A log, chopped by early travelers with a broad ax; scars rubbed on trees by wagons in passing; and a long section of the wagon-rutted trail itself.

The Washington State Federation of Women's Clubs began the park by donating the larger parcel of the total 612 acres in 1949 and added the rest later. The Interpretive Center, piped water, picnic grounds and tables, and the nature trails were made possible by bequest of Miss Catherine Montgomery, ardent conservationist and educator who died in 1958.

Pardon. There WAS a man in this picture too; a devoted forester and conservationist, Fred Cleator, who worked with the women to acquire and preserve this priceless opportunity to see our land with pioneer eyes.

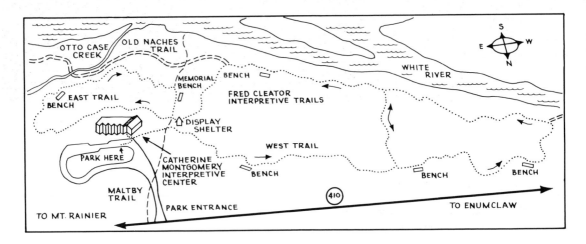

Trailside bench in Federation Forest State Park

Round trip approximately 1½ miles
Allow 2 hours
Best March to October, often good in winter
"Posh" trail: level, wide path and wagon road

74   SUN TOP LOOKOUT

Sun Top's attractions can be summed up in one word:
                            WOW!

Views are so spectacular we can say boldly, "Go!" There are no disappointed Sun Top hikers. A road goes all the way now. A trail can be seen in places but logging activities have spoiled its continuity. This excursion follows the final, steep ½-mile portion of trail. It SOUNDS short. Let me know when you come back!

Drive US 410 east from Enumclaw 24 miles to Snoqualmie National Forest boundary sign. About 1½ miles into the Forest, turn right from the highway onto Huckleberry Creek road No. 186. Pavement ends in .1 mile. Follow the gravel road past several forks to Sun Top road No. 188, which breaks left about 1½ miles from the highway. The narrow but good road climbs gradually at first through young timber, then steeply, in a hillside hug overlooking a sheer cliff. At 3000-foot elevation it changes to hard dirt. Switchbacks lift the traveler to expansive views. Across the valley the rocky escarpment of Noble Knob resembles a loaf of bread that has been cleaved through with a sharp knife. Logged patches on nearby hills look like frayed spots in green carpeting.

The last steep spurt above the spur road to Logging Area 10 reaches a saddle with plenty of parking space under a large seeding-project sign. Park here and begin the hike on the road which can be seen leading uphill to the lookout.

About 500 feet from the parking area watch for a trail, possibly marked by a small sign, on the left side of the road. The trail cuts straight across the hillside about 200 feet, then branches. Go right, uphill. One step at a time! The path winds through alpine wildflowers and huckleberries, and the feeling of being along with Julie Andrews in another SOUND OF MUSIC setting in the Swiss Alps makes the ascent by this route preferable to the road.

But before starting up, make a family pact. No one is to look over his shoulder and peek at the view until the top is reached. When the lookout is gained, turn around. The oh's and ah's blow up like balloons and pop as loudly. The view is . . . well . . . uttermost. From 5271 feet — a mile high — a complete 360-degree clean sweep. The Dalles, Crystal Mountain, Buck Creek, the Cascades, and west over Huckleberry Ridge to yet more ranges. Rainier's snow looks close enough to scoop off by hand; yet it is 15 airline miles distant and the tower here is almost 2 miles lower than Rainier's highest point.

To rest the eyes, note the old logs lying about the grassy knoll — so wind-eroded the grain stands out as though it had been sand-blasted.

Round trip 1 mile
Allow 2 hours
High point 5271 feet
Elevation gain 771 feet
Best May to October, often good later
Dirt road and trail

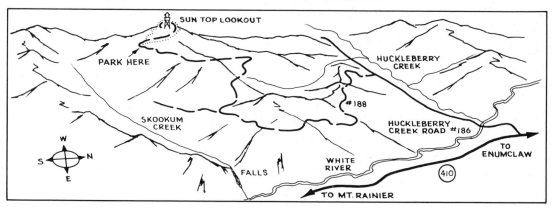

Mount Rainier from Sun Top Mountain

Carbon Ridge

75 CARBON RIDGE LOOKOUT

The Wilkes Expedition of 1841 bestowed the tongue-twisting name "Upthascap River" on one of Mount Rainier's major drainages. Later, when coal was discovered on its banks, somebody called it the Carbon River and the name stuck. Lucky for us? Only if ease of pronunciation is the criterion. "Upthascap" may lack poetry, but it has a lot of character.

Much of this hike lies in clearcut area, hot and grueling in summer sunshine. The best times are cool and breezy days in spring or fall — or overcast summer mornings when the expansive views can be expected to clear later on.

Carbon Ridge Lookout replaced nearby O'Farrell Lookout, and many maps still show only the name O'Farrell at both points. This hike covers both lookouts, which will clear up the puzzle.

Drive State 165 south from Puyallup through the old coal-mining town of Wilkeson (now best-known as the source of Wilkeson sandstone). At south end of town turn left on Railroad Avenue, paralleling, then crossing the tracks. The blacktop road ascends steeply a mile through cool woods above a gorge, changes to gravel, and 2 miles from town reaches Sunset Youth Camp. Then begins a 9-mile stretch of very rough, dirt road; definitely low-gear, full of deep chuckholes. Slow going, but pretty woods and not so

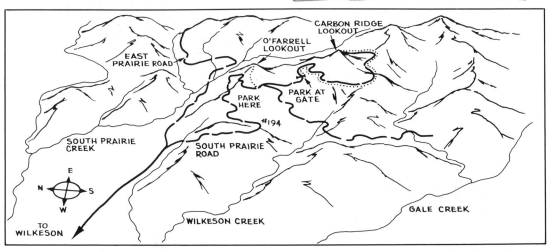

Coltsfoot growing through snow on Carbon Ridge

steep after the Camp. Huge firs alternate with stands of leafy maple and alder; big-leaf aralia blankets the road edge. About 3 miles from the Camp is a side-road to the left, but go straight ahead, following directions of a weathered sign, "O'Farrell L.O." (Road 194). About 8 miles from Sunset Camp a very rough, unmarked dirt lane takes off steeply uphill on the left. Park on the shoulder and hike ½ mile to the site of the old O'Farrell Lookout, a level knoll carpeted with daisies and ringed by firs. No trace remains of the tower, which burned years ago. Now drive ½ mile farther to a fork; sign points left to Carbon Ridge Lookout. Drive ½ mile more up the steep grade to a point where it dips to a yellow gate (usually open) just ahead of a switchback. Park beyond the gate, well off the road, and begin walking. The road is rocky around the turn, then changes to hard-packed dirt. Lowland views are great, looking north over Buckley and Enumclaw. An undependable trickle about 2 miles from the switchback is the only water supply, so carry a full canteen.

Ignore Section 16 Road, branching left about ½ mile from the gate. Stick right with "South Prairie Road" as it circles around the south side of the mountain, then shoots steeply the last ¼ mile for the top. The tower watches have been discontinued in favor of aerial patrol and the tower has been removed but views are wide from a spacious, level knoll dotted with stumps so weatherbeaten they look like polished silver. Only Rainier's crest can be seen lathering the top of Burnt Mountain.

The views missed on the climb up seem even better going down. The rounded humps of the Three Sisters to the northeast are prominent, and the green hills roll away into flatlands west of the Carbon and Puyallup Rivers far below.

Round trip 5½ miles (both lookouts)
Allow 4½ hours
High point 4144 feet
Elevation gain 1209 feet
Best May to October — often good later
Gravel-and-dirt road

Tolmie Creek forest road and Carbon valley

76   TOLMIE CREEK ROAD

Tolmie Peak and Tolmie Creek are somewhat lukewarm honors for a man who was one of the earliest explorers of the alpine Northwest, especially since he had nothing to do with either of them. The creek and the mountain on which it originates were named for Dr. William F. Tolmie, a Scotch surgeon who came to the Oregon country in 1833, fresh from medical school.

The hike along a logging road combines two very steep spurts with a level "breather" between. Superb views of the valley unfold like a map on the third lap. But this part is in clearcut, completely open and blazing in midsummer heat. The walk is ideal for a cool, rainy day, but views may be lost. Water is available (a bit difficult to get to) at a creek crossing halfway.

Drive south from Enumclaw or Puyallup to Buckley. Take State 165 south through Wilkeson and over Fairfax Bridge, spanning the spectacular Carbon River gorge. At a fork less than a mile from the bridge, go left on Carbon River entrance route into Mount Rainier National Park. Cross

Tolmie Creek, 7 miles from the fork, on concrete bridge and park on shoulder just beyond. Tolmie Creek road takes off on the right uphill.

The single-lane, rough gravel road is impossible to passenger cars so traffic is no problem. The way climbs steadily — 700 feet in a mile — through deep, second-growth woods with occasional glimpses of rampaging waters of the creek. At 1 mile a wide curve to the right, past a faint spur that goes straight up into the brush, brings one to a wooden bridge. Ptarmigan Ridge and Liberty Cap are just visible from here. When the magnetizing, plunging cascade can be left behind, cross the bridge and continue. The road, now smooth and level, hugs the hillside above the canyon. An old spar pole, still rigged with cables, is an interesting relic of logging days. In 1 mile from the bridge is a fork. The right is a dead-end spur to a loggers' landing. Stay left to start the second steep climb over loose rocks to a switchback where the road doubles left, then right.

A good place to end the hike (though the road continues) is another landing for logging operations that opens on the left to a wide shoulder 3/4 mile from the fork. Jumbles of bleached, weathered slash mark the spot. From this cliffside platform the Carbon River valley is spread below. Sand and gravel bars in the river, which looks sluggish from this height, are sur-prisingly clear and numerous. Views sweep west in a panorama clear to the Olympic Mountains across the Sound. From the road just above the spur, Mount Rainier, startlingly white and close, peers over the shoulder of Poch Peak. Other summits stand almost in staccato effect east along the river.

An avid natural scientist who was appointed factor of Hudson Bay Company's Fort Nisqually, Tolmie's journals are valuable references on the fur-trade period. He discovered coal outcroppings, identified certain of the region's flora and fauna, and was first to explore the Mount Rainier region on a botanizing expedition he made with five Indians into its northwest corner. He climbed a peak in the area, becoming the first white man to gain a close-up look at Rainier. Until recently it was thought he ascended the peak that bears his name, but new research indicates he actually climbed a ridge of Hessong Rock, several miles closer to The Mountain.

Round trip 5½ miles
Allow 4½ hours
High point 3800 feet
Elevation gain 2000 feet
Best April to October, often good later
Gravel road

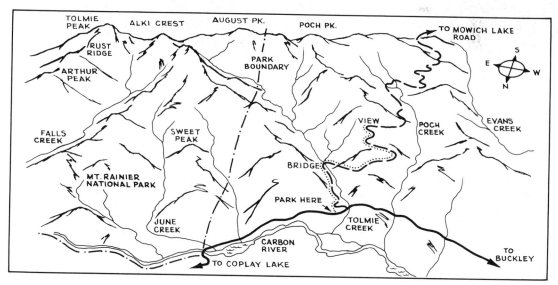

77   PUYALLUP RIVER

A river bank is a great antidote to "cabin fever" on a crisp, clear day when there's hardly time to reach mountains or seashore. Here is one near enough to home to offer the change of pace the doctor ordered: the exact prescription is up to you; the walk can be done in less than an hour or stretched to a day.

The Puyallup, like all of Puget Sound's rivers, has a distinctive character and personality — both shaped by man; first in "taming" it, then by utilizing its concrete banks to paint his own gaudy promotional ads.

Puyallup River and Mount Rainier

Wait for a day when the "Glory Mountain" can be seen, for the entire river road offers a thrilling sight of Rainier humped in silent reminder of the river's source — the Puyallup Glacier. Then hie south from Seattle on Interstate 5 to the exit marked "East Bay Street, Puyallup," just after the Port of Tacoma exit. (This is also **after** the exit marked "Puyallup.") Signs on the underpass lead on US 410 toward Puyallup. At the first bridge, about 3 miles, cross to the north side of the river and turn left. Continue to end of pavement and park where traffic is light.

Hike along this gravel road to its south end by the railroad bridge, then reverse. The river can be followed east all the way to Puyallup, 5 miles, if one likes. The south end by the railroad bridge may in future have inviting nature trails, if funds become available. Green fields add a quiet, pastoral tone; quail, pheasant, and even an occasional weasel can be seen.

The concrete revetments shaping the river's "character" were built in 1948 by U.S. Engineers and Inter-County Flood Control agencies, to keep the river from eroding its banks.

The hike passes through one of the Northwest's richest and most historic valleys. The town center, known, first as Franklin, was platted in 1877 by Ezra Meeker, a well-known pioneer who crossed the plains by covered wagon in 1852 and bestowed a new name — one he said would have no duplicate in the world. Newcomers have had difficulty pronouncing it ever since. The town became the center of rich pastures and berry fields, and later of canneries and wood-product plants. In 1906, when Meeker was 76, he retraced his old route across the nation by oxcart and wagon. Later he tried it by auto and in 1926, when he was 96, he flew over it by airplane.

Hike all the 5 miles to Puyallup and pay your respects to the intrepid pioneer at his statue in Pioneer Park. The public library occupies the site of his first log cabin home. Later, he built the 17-room mansion a few blocks away at 321 E. Pioneer Street. In 1970 the 82-year-old home almost went the way of bulldozing progress. But the Ezra Meeker Historical Society made a gallant, last-ditch stand to save the building; proudly saw success and its certification as a National Historic Site. You now can tour the lovely old mansion, restored and furnished as in Meeker's day, and see how it looked when he and his beloved Eliza Jane lived and reared their family of five (a sixth died young) children.

Round trip 1 to 10 miles
Allow 1 to 4 hours
Good all year
Paths and gravel-or-paved roads

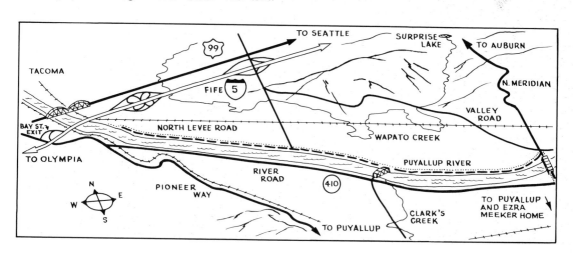

78   SPAR POLE HILL

From the park in Orting town center, search the crest of a hill lying straight south. The tall, lone pole that gives Spar Pole Hill its name can be seen stabbing the sky. Below it lie timberlands of the St. Regis Paper Company.

The hiker is welcome on a network of roads that winds through the company's forests for miles. But vehicles must be left at the gate. (Except hunting season. Stay away then!) Two routes will prime the thirst to explore for more: one short, the other very long. Expect plenty of company on the former, classed as prime grounds by mushroom hunters. In season, pickers are always out in force, especially after a heavy rain, with baskets, bags, even buckets and washtubs! The other is a pleasant woods hike along an easy old railway grade, with striking views from the namesake spar pole at the end.

Drive State 162 south from Puyallup through Orting to the Crocker Grange Intersection about a mile from town. Turn left, on South Prairie Road, then right about 1½ miles at a sign, "Voight Creek Gate." The paved road ascends slightly through close woods to a gate. Park here.

For the short hike, go left at fork above the gate. Three right turns at succeeding forks lead the hiker onto Windgate Road, then McDonald Road, and finally, from the last fork, on a short spur that deadends at a log blockade in the middle of deep, heavy, dank woods. Where the ground is covered by squirrel cone caches and their chomped-off peelings, thousands of Chantarelle mushrooms from pinhead to saucer size are nestled in a moss-and-fern blanket underneath the tress. Real Hansel-and-Gretel woods.

For the long hike, go right at first fork above gate, right again at another Y fork .6 mile (Fox Creek Road), and left at next fork, nearly 1 mile. Ignore a short spur next on the right, marked "Sparpole Road," and continue 1.7 miles farther. Turn right on a faint track marked "Beane Creek Road." The route of the old railway grade is overgrown with high grass but is distinct and wonderful hiking in a favorite deer-wintering area. The gradual climb soon brings views of Mt. Adams through the fringe of second growth.

Watch for an unmarked spur on the right which leaves the track at 2.2 miles and heads uphill in reverse direction. Follow it as it spirals steeply left through high grass and pearly everlasting ¼ mile to the crown of the hill. At road's end is the spar pole, a tall, dead snag still serving Nature's scheme as perch for a hawk. The pole was used in high-lead logging about 1910. Regeneration from that clearcut has been slow, but foresters are nursing hundreds of tiny firs,

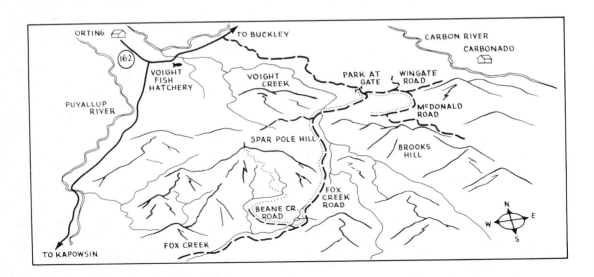

their long whips struggling to get above the nibbles of hungry deer.

Sidestep the young firs carefully and climb the low bank to the middle of the knoll for long-draught views: Enumclaw, Lake Tapps, Prairie Ridge, Tacoma, and Commencement Bay to the north; Carbonado below the eastern foothills; Mt. Rainier and Mt. Adams. In 20 years, if the baby trees get above the deer's jaws, those views again will be hidden.

Round trip: short hike, 3 miles; long hike, 12 miles
Allow 1½ hours for short; 6½ hours for long
High point (long hike) 1904 feet
Elevation gain 904 feet
Good all year, except in deep snow
Gravel and grass-grown road

Voight Creek on road to Spar Pole Hill

79   DOBBS MOUNTAIN

The Eatonville region was settled early by mountain emigrants from Tennessee, Kentucky, and the Carolinas who filled in the valleys around Alder to the southwest; by German homesteaders of the early 1880s who took land around Elbe, named for the German river; and by immigrants from the first wagon train who settled on the Yelm Prairie to the west. Eatonville was named for T. C. Van Eaton, who platted the townsite in 1888; later the town became an important lumber center.

This pleasant walk in a region logged during the 1920s follows a dirt road that tunnels through second-growth firs and gray-barked alder, bordered with ferns, devil's club, and vine maple, to a level viewing platform where Mount Rainier seems at finger-tip distance. A nice picnic spot, but carry water; there is none on the way. The road from the viewpoint continues down the south side of the mountain to National, an old logging town.

From Eatonville, follow the Elbe highway south and turn left on the Scott Turner Road at 2.7 miles. The paved road ascends between ranches outlined by rustic fenceposts and groves of alder that give way to firs and cedar. In 4 miles, pavement ends as the road swings right, below farmhouses. In another mile the graveled road narrows to a single lane where a post of an old gate remains, and weathered signs, long blotted out, once marked the road as built in the 1930s for forest protection. The road is for forest access only — meaning not an all-weather road. The rocky track is hard on tires and requires caution but is closed only during extreme fire hazard. In wet weather, passenger cars have been stuck in the mud.

Park at a turnout by the gate. The hike from here is 3½ miles to the lookout point; for a shorter walk, drive a mile farther to a wide spot near a white post.

The way ascends gently through woods that press close. The tranquility is soothing; the sun probes into cathedral-like arches of trees, and swarms of butterflies feather-dust the roadside thistles and rabbit brush. In fall, flaming vine maple look like spilled buckets of paint on the dark green hillside overlooking the Little Mashel River valley.

About 3 miles from the gate, suddenly the canyon seems to have transferred from right to left, and in another ¼ mile the road levels to an open clearing and a picture-window view of Mount Rainier.

Round trip from marked posts 7.2 miles
Allow 4 hours
High point 2750 feet
Elevation gain (from posts) 1000 feet
Best March to October
Rocky road

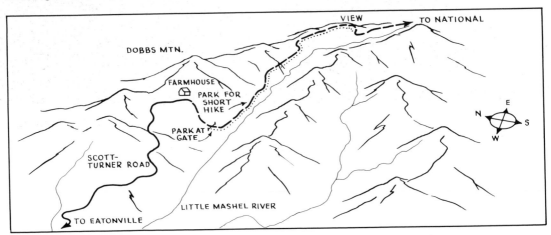

Mount Rainier from Dobbs Mountain

80   PACK FOREST: HUGO PEAK

Some of the loveliest walks available in Puget Sound lowlands are in the University of Washington Pack Forest near Eatonville. The 2200 acres of the College of Forest Resources's teaching-and-research grounds have miles of beautiful trails and roads. Formerly, roads were generally open for driving but budget restrictions and future extensive logging imposes control of access for safety, also possible relocation of trail access and routes. Watch for markers. If signs are posted or road gates closed DO NOT attempt to drive to shorten hikes. The reception for future visitors depends on your respect and good outdoor manners. No littering!

Drive west from Eatonville town center about 2½ miles to a junction with State 7. Turn left to Pack Forest entrance, marked by a large sign.

Stop at the gatehouse first. A stump is displayed of a tree that was 300 years old when Columbus discovered America. Then continue up the graveled road to a T intersection. Go left, away from camp buildings, and park in the saw-mill area, being careful not to block passageway to office and maintenance buildings.

For the first of three hikes in Pack Forest (see following pages for the others) begin by walking uphill 200 feet to another T intersection. This hike is a loop trip that begins and ends at this point. Turn left, past residences, to Lathrop Drive. Turn right through a gate.

Entrance to Pack Forest

The gravel lane is a pleasant, sunny-but-shaded level walk for a mile through young alder and maple, graced by a few firs and cedars and an occasional, chattering squirrel. Low hills and a valley open through a clearing on the left, then the view is hidden by a curtain of green. The logged hillside on the right is scattered with slash but fringed with new green. In 1½ miles, just past Reservoir Road spur, the curtain whisks away to reveal a small ravine on the left. Then the lane swings right in a wide curve south, with open, sunny fields and views toward Mt. Rainier.

Ascending gently, the way tunnels through deep woods and evergreens of ferns, blackberries, salal, and wildflowers, peppered with flashes of busy feathered creatures. After 2 miles, the ravine transfers to the right and at 2½ miles is a wide road junction, Kirkland Pass, the central point of Pack Forest and the beginning of hikes on following pages.

Turn right, on uphill road marked "Hugo Peak." The dirt lane climbs ½ mile among alder and ocean spray 140 feet higher to a dead-end among big trees, through which glimpses can be seen of the Olympic Mountains. Keep a sharp lookout halfway for a branch road and turn left on it. In a few feet a sign, "Camp Trail," marks the slightly-overgrown path which leads through forest along the edge of a gully, and in 1¼ miles drops off the hill onto the loop road. Turn right, back to the office buildings and car.

Before leaving Pack Forest, take one last, important stroll: Walk south from the sawmill past the camp buildings maintained for use of students. A simple monument, outside the dining hall, seems all the more eloquent in its open setting in a wide, green lawn. The inscription explains briefly:

"Charles Lathrop Pack, pioneer lumberman and conservationist, through whose interest and financial help the advancement of the Charles Lathrop Pack forest was initiated in 1925."

Round trip 4½ miles
Allow 2½ hours
High point 1740 feet
Elevation gain 640 feet
Good all year except deep snow
Gravel road, dirt trail

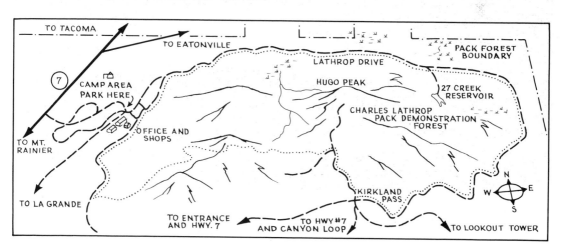

81   PACK FOREST: ECOLOGICAL AREA

A place where Nature has not been touched by the hand of man, where a forest of her most splendid giants has been allowed to stand and struggle for existence or fall and lie in tangled disarray and meld into Tomorrow and Tomorrow.

This is the "Ecological Area" in the University of Washington Pack Forest, one of the few "raw nature" walks existing in lowlands hereabouts. The trail through this area, called the "fun trail" by professors and students of the University's College of Forest Resources, passes two groups of huge trees several hundred years old. The large specimens survived a fire 200 years ago; the rest of the stand has regenerated since then.

Follow the directions in Hike 80 to Pack Forest and to Kirkland Pass. The Ecological Area hike is short, in marked contrast to the Lookout Tower trip (Hike 82); both can be done the same day. (If gate is clearly open to public access, you may want to drive and park at the Pass if time is short.)

The Ecological Area was set aside as an essential part of forestry studies, showing the interrelationship of organisms and plants with their environment, and what transpires when an area is left to itself, unmanaged by man.

Find the wide, needled path that leads downhill between the big trees opposite the Hugo Peak road. In about 100 steps the path divides. Follow either branch; they unite again in 600 feet. The right, however, marked in a few feet by a sign, "Trail of the Giants," is the most impressive.

Feeling suddenly dwarfed, the stroller threads among huge trees to a gully, where an enormous Douglas fir stands on a sort of pedestal, itself 3 feet above the forest floor. Look to the left of the big tree for steps easing the path down into the gully and up the other side to meet the other trail branch. Continue downhill. Patched with clumps of vanilla leaf and deer fern, the way follows along the gully, which grows steadily to canyon size, piled high with jumbles of downed trees. The place is populated by giants, standing or fallen. One climbs over 6-foot-thick logs on carved steps, and walks 100 feet along the top of a log slightly shaved to level the "path." (This IS the hand of man but the only touch.)

About ½ mile down into the gorge "The Witness Tree," marked by a sign, indicates the original tree used in surveying to show a corner, and the snafu that resulted when difficulties were experienced working across the canyon. The survey was not accepted; a few years later another was made. The small map made for distribution by the office shows a jog and two corners at the spot where the mixup resulted.

Beyond the Witness Tree, the trail continues down the gorge ½ mile. Returning on the path, soft and resilient with needles, the hiker bursts out on the road at Kirkland Pass as though coming up from a nether world and, startled, realizes the most impressive and outstanding feature of this entire stroll has been the utter, Elysian silence.

Round trip 1 mile (Add 6 to Kirkland Pass and return)
Allow 1 hour
High point 1600 feet
Elevation gain 225 feet
Good all year, except deep snow
Dirt path

Douglas fir along the Pack Forest nature trail

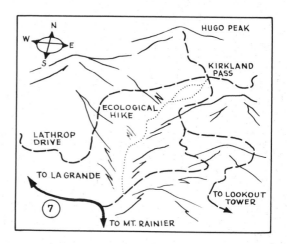

82 PACK FOREST: LOOKOUT TOWER LOOP

The third hike on the network of roads and trails in the University of Washington Pack Forest reaches the highest point of the Forest, offering a pleasant, sun-dappled walk between banks of ferns and big-leaf aralia shielded by young alder.

Follow the previous directions to Pack Forest and Kirkland Pass. Begin the hike on the road south from the pass, opposite the Hugo Peak road. The way descends sharply through close woods of alder, with glimpses of a gorge, and in ½ mile reaches a Y fork. Go left. The gravel road climbs gradually above a deepening canyon on the right. Views are spare, screened by the wall of green.

In 1 mile, turn right on a branch road, possibly unmarked. This road, leading to the "Canyon Loop," is smooth and pleasant walking, with little grade, and reaches a T intersection in ½ mile. Go either direction to loop back to the T. Between timber stands are views of Alder Dam and Lake to the south.

Return to the main road and continue the climb, sticking left past a branch, timber access road, which dead-ends. Several buildings, almost hidden in brush on the left at about 1¾ mile from Kirkland Pass, mark the lookout tower rising 70 feet above the road. A gravel path from the road leads to the metal tower. For acrophobes like this writer, the tower seems shaky and a bit fearsome. Try at least two or three flights, then hang on for some of the best views in the countryside. Mt. Rainier stares back, close enough to touch, towering over baby foothills like a hen over chicks.

A swing of the head (careful now!) reveals the Olympic Mountains to the west. Southward, below the tower, better views now of sparkling Lake Alder, behind Alder Dam.

From the tower, continue the road as it loops just under 1 mile back to Kirkland Pass. This segment of the loop is shorter and steeper than the approach; the trees grow bigger, the canyon deeper and views broader.

From Kirkland Pass, head west on Lathrop Drive, which circles south, then north, to return to the Pack Forest camp buildings and entrance.

Along this route interesting plantings are marked, intriguing enough to bid the hiker return some day: stands of Port Orford Cedar and Western Red Cedar planted in 1928. Below, out of sight of the road, a planting of Ponderosa pine makes a fascinating "race study" watched closely by forestry students. Seeds of the pine taken from many different states, ranging from Arizona to Oregon to North Dakota, were planted in 1928, to illustrate the importance of seed sources.

Round trip 4¾ miles (Add 6 to
  and from Kirkland Pass)
Allow 3 hours
High point 2000 feet
Elevation gain 400 feet
Good all year except deep snow
Gravel road

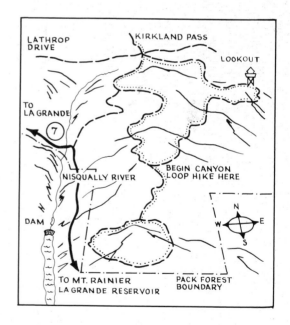

Road in Pack Forest

Bald Hill Lake

83   BALD HILL LAKE

Moonshine country. That's the Bald Hills. Old records tell us they were the favorite haunt of moonshiners before the repeal of the Volstead Act.

Several hills or hill-clusters around Elbe and Alder bear the name Bald. Was it a canny ruse of the booze-brewers to lead pursuing revenuers a merry chase? One Bald Hill in Thurston County walls off the town of Alder from Bald Hill Lake.

Drive Interstate 5 south and exit at "Mount Rainier-Puyallup" sign. Continue south through Puyallup on State Highway 161 to Eatonville, then right (west) from the junction at town center 3 miles to paved State Highway 7 and turn left. (For an alternate route take State 7 from South Tacoma through Parkland and Spanaway to this point.)

At the junction on State 7, drive slowly a short distance and watch for an overpass. Go under it; turn immediately left on a dirt access road to the overpass above the paved highway and turn left on a gravel logging road (R 7). Follow it on a long grade down to a bridge across the Nisqually River, then up another long grade. About 8 miles watch for a sign, "Bald Hill Lake," on the left (east). (If sign is gone a paved highway is ¼ mile beyond the turn-off point.) At a fork ¼ mile on the lake road, turn left again on a short, rocky, uphill track and in ½ mile turn right to the Weyerhaeuser picnic and campground area on a slope above the lake. Water and facilities are available on the assumption one minds his outdoor manners.

One can imagine liquor stills operating furtively in the woods rimming the edge of this small (45-acre) eerie-looking lake, an excellent example of a body of water being consumed by phreatophytes (plant life) and not one to entice swimmers. Stagnant, murky, almost every inch all the way to the opposite shore is crammed with water lilies and plants.

Two short, varied hikes take one almost to the same point on the east side. Find a trail back of the big cedar tree about 50 feet behind and to the right of the dock. It is overgrown but well-defined and not difficult. Past big boulders, over and under fallen logs, the trail skirts the south shore about ¾ mile where it climbs along a rocky ledge for a good view about 30 feet above the lily-choked lake, ending there at a deep cleft.

Return to the picnic area for the second hike and follow the dirt road north into the trees, around the west shore, in and out of sunbeams and shade to the north-end boat launch, about ¾ mile. A Boy Scout trail can be seen over the hump of the cliff abutting the road-end; a good guide is needed to follow this path, which leads to hard cliffside scrambling.

This strangely-intriguing area invites one to sit quietly and study marsh life — bugs, frogs, and birds by the hundreds. Big grouse flush from the thickets inland, marsh birds croon softly before they flap off heavily in alarm, and land birds peck busily at seeds and berries from trees and brush, ignoring the hiker as he pads softly along road or trail.

Round trip 3 miles
Allow 3 hours
High point 663 feet
Good all year; best spring and summer when
   lilies bloom
Dirt trail

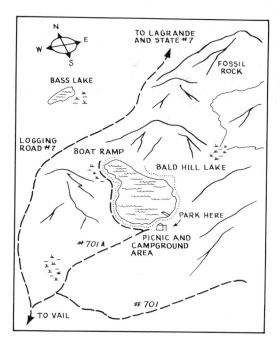

Swan Creek

84   SWAN CREEK CANYON

There's something about a hole in the earth. Give a child a shovel and set him loose in a sandpile or vacant lot: he sets happily to digging.

Any gouge has a fascination, and the affinity carries to adulthood. Swan Creek Canyon, a wooded ravine and stream in Tacoma, is one of Nature's gouges that invites indulging in the primitive urge to poke deep.

Drive Interstate 5 to exit marked "East Bay

186

Street, Puyallup." Follow signs for Puyallup highway. Just beyond Indian Mission Center, turn on Pioneer Way, which angles right. In a mile, near a junction with Waller Road, a Pierce County Park sign marks a gravel jeep road. Park and walk the path across the field. It leads, in ½ mile, to a small waterfall, then dwindles to a trail beyond—a hike of another mile or two, depending on creek level. The County and Fisheries Service cooperated to reinstate the salmon run by stocking fish· and installing a fish ladder at the waterfall — for education as well as recreation.

Variety and abundance are seen in the canyon's different habitats. Shrubs of wild rose, dogwood, mahonia, hazelnut, spirea, honeysuckle, syringa; and among wildflowers, buttercup, lily, trillium, solomon's seal, bleeding heart, violet, foxtail, columbine, coral-root. Fresh greens are in the creek — miner's lettuce and watercress. Indians and settlers gathered plants from this canyon for food. Of birds, nesting and migrant, 28 species are seen, from hummingbirds to hawks, ducks to pheasant. Not to mention the woodsy folk from mice and chipmunks to deer.

For an east-side hike through a gravel pit, drive on Waller Road south and uphill from the junction with Pioneer Way. Opposite house number 5017 is an entrance road into a gravel pit marked "No Shooting." Park off the road by the fence and begin hiking toward the right.

Let the children unwind their springs in the vast pit, then walk to the northwest corner marked by an old dynamite shack. Above the shack, at the edge of another clearing, a trail leads left into the canyon and down to the creek at bottom. An old road can be traced faintly along the shelf above the creek.

The music of the chattering creek plays a happy tune to your steps — a pocket of beauty now to be enjoyed, where once its destiny was an open cesspool. Once used indiscriminately for a garbage dump, the canyon was rescued through a timely loan by The Nature Conservancy, cooperating with city and county agencies. The land is owned by Pierce County and is part of a joint project with the City of Tacoma in developing a park of more than 200 acres. Plans are to maintain it as a natural science laboratory and center for teaching and research in flora, fauna, and geology.

Round trip (two hikes) 3 to 5 miles
Allow 2 to 3 hours
Good all year
Dirt road and trail

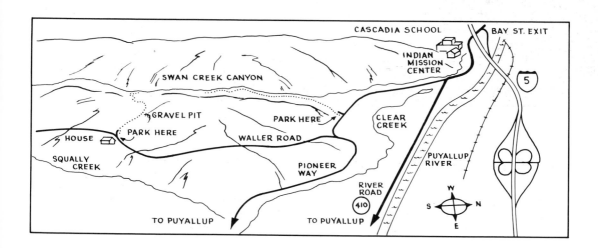

85 COMMENCEMENT BAY

Commencement Bay is to Tacoma what Elliott Bay is to Seattle. This hike from downtown Tacoma up the hill fronting the bay is like ascending an elevator rising above the genesis of the city — where Tacoma history began. True, the picture is drastically changed from the forest-clad hills and mudbanks of the quiet natural harbor seen by the first explorer, Captain George Vancouver in 1792. The bay was christened 49 years later when the Wilkes Expedition began surveys there.

In Tacoma, drive north on Pacific Avenue to 10th Street and turn right. The one-way street ends on Cliff Avenue which descends on the right to parking areas under the 11th Street Bridge. Begin the walk by retracing to A Street and go north. At 9th Street, by the police station, is Tacoma's famous totem pole made by Alaska Indians.

Continue on A Street to the Allied Arts Building and museum on Seventh Street, a dressed-up portion of an old Annex to the historic Tacoma City Hall across Pacific Avenue, which historians are trying to preserve, complete with clock tower and chimes. A bridge conducting traffic quickly uphill to Stadium Way, our objective, is too dangerous for pedestrians. Go straight on Seventh to Commerce Street and turn right. It merges soon with Stadium Way.

Majestic views on the gradual ascent: Puget Sound sweeps northwest around Point Defiance;

beyond is the Olympics' jagged crest. Eastward, the flats of Puyallup River and meandering creeks spread from numerous industrial piers and terminals to the Cascade Range with its bulky star, Mt. Rainier (or should we say, "Mt. Tahoma?") Below in the harbor, freighters load and unload cargo; tugs puff as they tow long log rafts; fishing craft freckle the waters between while gulls wheel and scream as they keep alert for goodies dumped from galleys.

At the time that pioneers Denny, Boren, and Bell were staking claims on Seattle's downtown streets in 1852, Nicholas De Lin, a Swede, was clearing land for the first sawmill at a junction of two creeks near present-day railroad lines. De Lin and his family fled to the fort for safety during the Indian uprising in the White River valley, then returned to work the mill until 1861. Then came Job Carr, to build a log cabin on his homestead at Chebaulip, or Old Town. And after him promoter McCarver, who renamed the settlement Tacoma. From then on, Tacoma "just growed."

Where Stadium Way momentarily becomes lost at the intersection of North E Street and North 1st Street, continue west on North E Street, past the impressive "natural" stadium next to Stadium High School — an enormous natural gorge ingeniously buttressed with concrete walls and filled with bleachers. Turn right off North E Street on the other side of the stadium to pick up Stadium Way again. In one block is the State Historical Museum, well worth a full afternoon's browsing. Continue on Stadium Way 5 blocks to

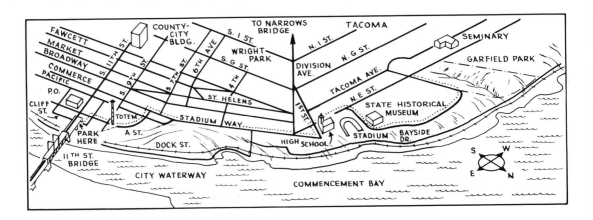

Commencement Bay

Borough Road, bordering Garfield Park. A green lawn at the park's south end holds a treasure of memories. The elite of the Gay Nineties gathered here, strolling paved walks radiating from a concert pavilion. Only iron bases of former beautiful lamp standards remain as scant testimony of "dear old days." On moonlit nights, paths leading down the gorge to the water were well-populated. Now the gorge is partly filled in and reshaped in a brave new park plan with new trails. One wonders: will the moonlight strolls be any better?

Round trip 4 miles
Allow 2½ hours
Good all year
Paved sidewalks

Puget Sound from Point Defiance

86   POINT DEFIANCE PARK

I first noticed him as I set out to explore a trail which beckoned from the woods. His smile was wide and friendly. From this veteran hiker I learned to appreciate the best of Point Defiance Park.

For 10 years this young and vibrant 75-year-old, Edwin A. Glueck, has hiked his favorite route of 5 miles through the park every day, rain or shine. His soft, unhurried tread on the forest path sets no creature scurrying, for he has a nodding acquaintance with nearly every wild deer, fox, porcupine, raccoon, and squirrel who share his beloved woods. He knows every "squirrel warehouse" — where mounds of seed cones have been piled and picked over by groups of the bushy-tails in community "chomp-ins." Regularly, every 2 weeks, he checks to see if his friend, a bald eagle, awaits his visit perched on a favorite snag. And at the end, he greets the zoo animals, who give every sign they look forward to his daily visit — a familiar face among so many strange ones.

To him, we owe our hike around the point and back to the zoo, which he traced in detail.

Follow signs through downtown Tacoma west via signs to Point Defiance Park. First-time visitors to the park may not finish the various attractions of zoo, aquarium, Fort Nisqually, Never Never Land, and the Forest Industries Museum with the restored logging camp and old-time skidder. But a full day will allow for such visits plus the hike.

Park drives are all one-way, radiating in a series of ever-widening circles. The zoo and aquarium are on the shortest, inner loop; the others are on the second loop and a "5-mile view drive" swings around the outer edge for views.

For our hike, turn left at the first fork for the aquarium and park in the lot below. Then walk uphill a few feet above the entrance road and pick up a blacktop road opposite the new aviary building. In a few steps, two trails can be seen. Take the right. The trail, through a "natural cathedral," as our old friend describes it, skirts a gulch and exits in ¼ mile on the paved outer loop road.

Turn left on the pavement to cross the gulch and resume path on other side, left of pavement. In 50 feet the trail veers to the right and later forks. Keep right. The trail crosses the loop road and in a few steps the paved, return road from Owens Beach, then resumes as a footpath. This winds around, returning to the

"5-mile" pavement near a yellow-and-red fire hydrant, No. 22. Cross pavement, follow trail downhill and over open country. Three dirt roads cross the trail, which now becomes narrow and a bit overgrown just before it finally comes to the picnic grounds at the point. You have now walked about 2 miles.

Land's end here is atop a 200-foot cliff with a most-rewarding seascape. Dwarfed sailboats, tugs, barges, and motorboats chug past your toes as you gaze over Dalco Passage northeast to Vashon Island and across the beginning of the Narrows to Gig Harbor and other parts of Great Peninsula beyond.

To return, walk past lookout tower almost to fire hydrant No. 36 and pick up a trail into woods. A dead snag near the hydrant is the perch to which the bald eagle, mentioned earlier, returns every other week to meet our ever-vigorous hiker.

At a fork about 15 feet from the road, take a right turn. Trail continues about a mile, then crosses two paved branches of the second loop highway (which proceeds to Never Never Land). Keep on the wooded trail on left side of this highway, leading back to the zoo and aquarium in about 3 miles.

Round trip 5 miles
Allow 2 hours
Good all year
Dirt trail

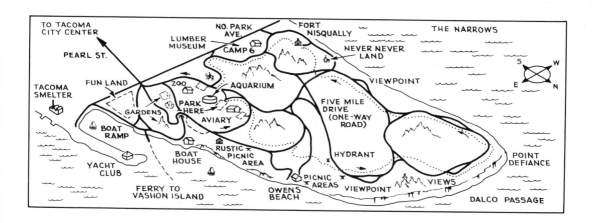

87   STEILACOOM

No city in the Puget Sound area, save for Port Townsend, still wears the patina of pioneer days and exudes an atmosphere of the past as does Steilacoom. You go backward in time with each step in this oldest incorporated town on Puget Sound. But hurry, for modern homes now jostle the old; soon the charm of old pewter will be rubbed off by neon and chrome.

Drive south on Interstate 5 to exit west marked "Steilacoom" (north of Ft. Lewis) and continue about 8 miles, past shopping centers and Western State Hospital. These extensive grounds were the early beginning of Fort Steilacoom, begun as a farm by Joseph Heath, English settler. Opposite the main gate of the hospital is a stone pyramid which marks the military road to Walla Walla.

The road narrows, swooping and twisting downhill through woods of alder and fir. A large sign marks entrance to Steilacoom, where Starling Street begins at Cedar Street. Park near here and continue on foot in same direction.

Steilacoom, said to be named after an Indian chief, "Tail-a-koom," (also called "Chilicum" and "Chelacoom") was founded by Captain Lafayette Balch when he was miffed at high land prices in Olympia. It sprouted stores and homes like mushrooms even before it was incorporated in 1854. Five years later it boasted 70 homes and numerous shops, as well as many Puget Sound "firsts" — jail, Protestant Church, courthouse, and mills. This stroll along four streets passes some of these historic sites.

At Union Avenue, which dips down to a ferry dock serving Anderson Island, double back and go in opposite direction on the next street (Rainier). Reaching Cedar, go downhill to Lafayette, walk to Union and reverse again on the last street, Commercial.

Not all sites can be listed, but here — grouped by streets — are enough to spur you to find the rest:

Starling: Between Main and Balch, first Territorial Jail, built 1858, torn down 1944.

At Main, look uphill one block. At Nisqually is Catholic Church, built 1857 at Fort Steilacoom and moved here 1864.

Rainier: Before turning back on Rainier, look across Union. On Martin between 6th and 7th was first county courthouse, 1854, now gone. Proceed north.

At Main, look downhill toward Lafayette, east side. Behind a tall, 100-year-old maple was the first wagon shop, built 1875, changed now with false front gone. On its left is an old barn, about 1910. On its right the Nathaniel Orr home, built 1857.

Lafayette: Longest electric line in the world (13 miles) for a time. In operation 1889 to 1916.

Bair Drug Store, corner Wilkes. Built 1895. Still in use at this writing, but sagging with age. At rear of store, outside, is monument with bell on top, now rung for fires, marking site of first Protestant Church north of Columbia River. Built 1853.

Town Hall and Visitors Center at Main. Small museum with splendid display of old photographs. Map of town may be purchased.

At Union: Sign marking military road, built in time to provide escape inland from Indian massacre, 1855.

Commercial: (All buildings demolished or moved with coming of Northern Pacific Railway, 1912.)

At Wilkes: Northwest corner, Masonic Temple, 1860.

At Main: North side, site of two-story log house, erected 1852, where first public school classes held; also refuge during Indian war. Almost opposite is restored old mansion built 1858.

Between Balch and Puyallup, south side was first brick store; on north side, butcher shop (1850), postoffice, livery stable, saloon.

At foot of Puyallup, blacksmith shop, run by one of first soldiers who landed, 1849.

Round trip 2 miles
Allow 2 hours; 5 if a history buff and museum is open
Good anytime
Paved streets

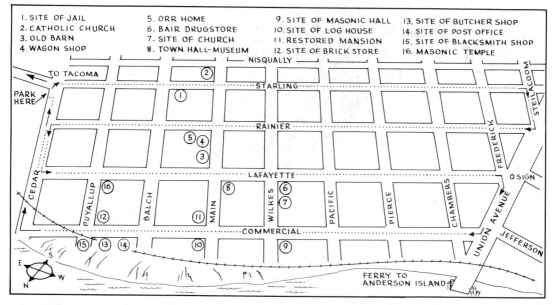

1. SITE OF JAIL
2. CATHOLIC CHURCH
3. OLD BARN
4. WAGON SHOP
5. ORR HOME
6. BAIR DRUGSTORE
7. SITE OF CHURCH
8. TOWN HALL–MUSEUM
9. SITE OF MASONIC HALL
10. SITE OF LOG HOUSE
11. RESTORED MANSION
12. SITE OF BRICK STORE
13. SITE OF BUTCHER SHOP
14. SITE OF POST OFFICE
15. SITE OF BLACKSMITH SHOP
16. MASONIC TEMPLE

Restored home at Steilacoom

88 NISQUALLY RIVER

The Nisqually River area fairly sighs with history. It was the Happy Hunting Ground of the Nisqually Indians; Fort Nisqually, near the river's mouth, was built in 1833; the luxuriant delta grasses supported the Northwest's first cattle herds; and the area furnished the wedge by which the first Americans, who settled in 1839, spelled the end of the Hudson Bay Company's domain in the Northwest.

On this hike along the Nisqually River, people the meadows beside the singing waters with those early creators of our history. At the end is a surprise dividend.

From Interstate 5 just south of Fort Lewis take exit "Mounts Road-Old Nisqually." Go east from overpass descending the maple-lined road 3.3 miles. Cross bridge and turn left on first road at sign, "Public Fishing." Park at dead-end by river, marked for fishermen. Trails fan out from road's end here, but head for the huge concrete support of the railroad trestle and bear left on a trail to the riverbank. Continue upriver through thick underbrush strung with gossamer curtains of spider webs to a log jam with a backwash pool. Keep riverside where the path splits. Ahead, where two great boles sprout from a single trunk, an enormous log jam almost dams the river — a gossip mart for birds. From trunk to trunk they fly over the tangled mass and trade their news before leaving for home, their bills laden with goodies.

The path leaves the river, goes into woods and in ½ mile meets a gated jeep road flanking the railroad embankment. Turn left. The road continues almost a mile, peaceful and lovely under maples and water-loving willows and cottonwood. A flat-top boulder along the way is an ideal spot for a picnic.

The jeep track joins Durkin Road where it tunnels under the high railroad embankment. The arch at the far tunnel entrance bears the date 1912. Turn left on Durkin Road for the surprise: an enormous, gnarled cedar tree on the left — 11 feet thick, 170 feet tall, almost bald of greenery. Guess its size and age. Look carefully — is there something unusual about it?

Before the Pilgrims landed on our shores,

before Joan of Arc was burned at the stake, before the Magna Carta was signed, this tree, estimated to be 800 to 1200 years old, was reaching for the sun. The compact road gravel, close to its buttress roots, almost killed it. But our aged friend counteracted — sending up three large branches on its opposite side. The topmost branch can be seen as an unusual natural graft, welded to BOTH the main trunk and the branch below it. Trees, too, have fighting spirit!

What changes this grizzled veteran has seen! No matter where one walks in this valley is historic ground. Chief Leschi pastured his horses on ranges just across the river where now is heard the sound of guns from Fort Lewis firing ranges, and Indian longhouses stood nearby.

The jeep track beside the railroad can be followed all the way back to the car; for variety, hike under the tunnel and past a large gravel works to the highway. This adds .8 mile to the total. Turn right on the highway. A stone monument at the Nisqually Valley Ranch Market pays homage to the Medicine Creek Treaty. Chief Leschi, who refused to sign what he considered a betrayal of his people, would have other thoughts about that!

Round trip (returning by highway) 3.8 miles
Allow 2½ hours
Good all year except flood season
Dirt path and road

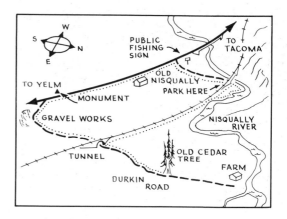

Old cedar tree near Nisqually River

State Capitol and Capitol Lake

89   CAPITOL LAKE

One view the westward-bound freeway traveler through Olympia cannot fail to notice, no matter what his speed, is the Capitol dome, towering 278 feet into the sky, its mirrored image shimmering in the water at its base.

Many Washingtonians have toured their Capitol buildings, but few go beyond to explore Capitol Lake. This man-made lake has transformed mudflats to a picture-postcard setting and provided a recreational playground.

Follow the street at the north end of the Capitol grounds, beside the Administration Building, continue downhill and park on the lake shore near warehouses, where a large, new paved lot has been provided for visitors. The youngsters will be attracted — perhaps diverted — by a children's park to the north of the lot, with its "Jungle Jim," swim areas, picnic tables and concessions, but head them south first. The once-barren look of our first visits has been softened by a line of 86 flowering cherry trees along the shore. About .1 mile, at the foot of the bluff, is the Northern Pacific Railway line. Cross it and continue around the bluff, where the walkway dead-ends by an old gray building with a tall smokestack that pokes above the top of the bluff. This is the heating plant for the Capitol buildings.

From the platform here is a good view of the lake. Cinched near the middle like an hourglass by the railroad trestle, the waters billow north and south to provide hundreds of acres for aquatic sports.

Return to the parking area. (Do NOT try to cross the lake on the narrow trestle; train movements are frequent and unscheduled.) Continue beyond the car, hugging the lake on Water Street, Fifth Avenue West, then left on Deschutes Parkway.

It is a trifle over a mile from the car to the other end of the railroad trestle, on a boulevard lined with stately Lombardy poplars; in gathering dusk the way is particularly lovely, the lights of the Capitol buildings reflecting in the lake. Another mile alongside the lake ends the hike at the freeway overpass.

The fresh-water lake is the result of a new idea in landscaping and scenic attractions. Formerly the salt water entered the cove from Budd Inlet and an unsightly spread of mudflats was the unphotogenic part of the postcard Capitol group scene. In 1949 a dam was constructed, with a concrete spillway across the neck of Budd Inlet. The salt water was allowed to go out with the tide, then the gate was permanently shut. The sparkling fresh water pouring from the Deschutes Falls filled the area behind the dam and the boulevard now is a scenic drive.

More plans are in store by the City Parks and Recreation Department: a walkway completely encircling the lake; islands in its center; connecting bridges.

Round trip 3-2/3 miles
Allow 3 hours
Good anytime
Gravel path and pavement

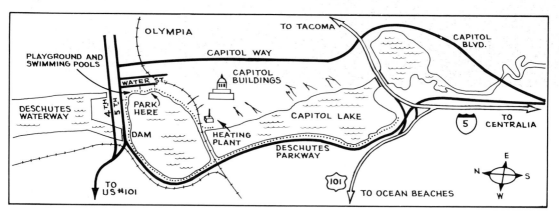

90   TUMWATER

When Colonel Michael T. Simmons and his 32 weary companions finished their cross-country journey in 1845 and picked a cascading river above Budd Inlet for the first American colony north of the Columbia River, they labeled their settlement "Newmarket." Practical, and typically American; obviously there would be heavy commerce with Fort Nisqually, the leading port of clearance for trade on Puget Sound. Happily, the Indians' name for the falls — Tumtum, meaning throb of the heart — suggested by the drumming sound of the waterfalls, persists today though anglicized in part. Tumwater has a wonderful sound.

Unlike Steilacoom, not much remains to

Tumwater Falls

suggest those early days except a surprise feature — the Crosby house, built in 1854.

Drive Interstate 5 south to Tumwater exit (after the one marked "State Capitol"). The Olympia Brewery is on the left (east). Turn toward it at intersection, cross the freeway, then go right again, passing Terrace Falls Restaurant to the Tumwater Park entrance. Leave the car in the park and begin the walk on the restaurant side of the falls. Before descending the inclined path, examine the interesting petroglyph display — including a huge boulder from Harstine Island — at the rear corner of the park office building.

Below the restaurant by the path is a granite monument commemorating the first American settlers. Continue under the bridge which leads to the modern brewery. (Accept the invitation to tour — 8 to 4:30 daily — **after** the hike, when properly thirsty).

If music soothes the savage breast, Tumwater Falls could calm a grizzly. The walk down one side of the Deschutes River and back up the other is in rhythm to an aquatic symphony: the swish, gurgle, trickle, splash, rush, and roar between three falls of tumbling, clear water. Rockery plantings around small rock pools under cascades, banked with ivy, add visual beauty to the liquid melodies. Stop and listen often — on an "orchestra seat" rock ledge over the churning rapids (take steps at end of a long footbridge halfway down) or a picnic table below the path farther along, or a platform at the last falls

(Deschutes Falls), where you can see the old brewery at the head of Capitol Lake before crossing to the other side for return. The plant was first built of wood in 1905 and 1907. Washington went dry in 1916; the old plant was used for a time to bottle fruit juices, then sold to a paper-manufacturing company. The new brewery was constructed in 1933.

Return to the restaurant and circle around to its entrance. Stay on the same street and walk straight across the intersection with the bridge. Downhill, in a green triangle behind where the road curves to the left (.3 mile) is the Crosby house, white with green shutters and ornate fretwork edging the roof. The house was built in 1854 by Bing Crosby's grandfather, Nathaniel Crosby III, an early-day settler who ran a gristmill and sawmill on the Deschutes River. Maintained by the Daughters of the Pioneers, it is open to visitors on Thursday afternoons.

To return, follow a dirt road on the right to the lake shore, with an even better view of the old brewery across the lake. The dirt road returns to the restaurant and the park, paralleling the paved road leading to the Crosby house.

Round trip 1 mile
Allow 1 hour (not including brewery or house tours)
Good anytime
Dirt path

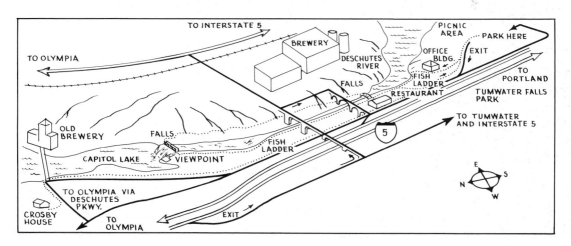

State Capitol (telephoto) and Olympia waterfront from Priest Point Park

91 PRIEST POINT PARK

To the place of the gigantic firs holding the secret sepulchres of the Squaxin Indians came Father Pascal Ricard, an Oblate priest, to build his order's first mission in the New World, in 1848. The mission and the Indian burial canoes lodged in the treetops have disappeared, but the forest giants remain, preserved as a public park. The 254-acre park still is only partially developed, but two hikes — a woods trail and a beach walk — give a taste of more to come.

Drive Interstate 5 south to "Olympia" exit (just before the one marked "State Capitol"). From exit ramp continue straight on Plum Street, which leads onto East Bay Drive, going north. At 2½ miles, turn into first park entrance road on the right, after a large park sign on Mission Road. Drive to parking area near the maintenance buildings.

The forest trail begins north of the restrooms and shop buildings, dips to a small foot-bridge, then follows a small gully to a fork. Here is the first in a network of loops that intertwine through woods. Going left from this fork deposits one at the park's outer rim. But the right branch leads to another fork, then another, then still more, depending on the route one chooses. A wooded hide-and-seek in a forest mosaic of wild ginger and salal, ferns and Oregon grape, under enormous hemlocks, maples, cedars, and firs. And no worries about getting lost, as long as the hiker stays on a trail. Paths lead either to circumference roads or back to the start. Greater stretches of primitive woods wait future trail-builders at the north end. There one CAN get lost until trails are built.

For a beach hike, continue north on East Bay Drive past a Y split with Ames Road (keep left) about .6 mile. Turn left on Flora Vista Road. Immediately after, turn left again on a hard-packed gravel road on the left that wanders through woods. Drive a few yards to the first wide spot and park. Take lunch and water; many inviting picnic spots will appear. Hike down the road .3 mile to a wide turnout that circles around some trees. (The road continues from here but stops high above the beach with no way down.) Find the trail almost opposite, slightly left of the turnout. It is overgrown (Park Department plans include improvement) and may be damp; crow caws sound like laughter as one brushes aside brambles and steps over fallen trunks, but the trail is distinct and short, about 700 steps to the beach. Mark the trail exit immediately with sticks or obvious sign to help find it on return.

Turn left (south). Across Budd Inlet, above the cityscape, the Capitol Dome can be seen. The shore strip cuts sharply inland to round the long finger of Ellis Cove, then west again where, at 1 mile, it underlines the bluff and lawns forming the main picnic and recreation area of the park. Mudflats halfway, at the inner reach of the cove, may make walking the entire distance difficult, however. If so, return to the trail exit and go north ¼ mile, where private dwellings mark the park boundary, for the finish.

On the return, don't miss more seascapes and cityscapes from the viewing platform in the main picnic area. Turn toward the water opposite the entrance for the woods hike. For a look at the site of the first mission, drive or walk on Mission Drive to water's edge. Nothing remains but the location and a faint aura. Here sat the "dark monastery, surrounded by gardens and fragrant wallflowers." Across the road was the long shed or "wash-house" used as a school for Indian boys, whose ancestors slept in peace in their burial canoes high in nearby treetops.

Only 120 years ago.

Round trip: woods, 1-2 miles; beach, 2 miles
Allow 4 hours
Good all year
Forest path and pebbled beach

Nature trail, Priest Point Park

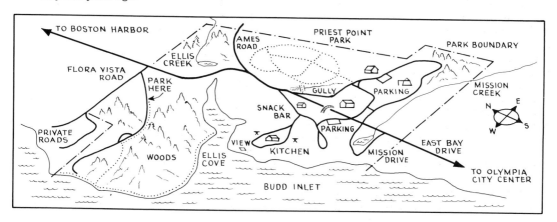

92   ROCK CANDY MOUNTAIN

Don't expect a "lemonade spring, where bluebirds sing; hens that lay softboiled eggs, bulldogs with rubber teeth, and a lake of booze where you can paddle around in big canoes," as described in the folk song made popular by Burl Ives.

Records are scarce on whether OUR Rocky Candy Mountain, in the Black Hills west of Olympia, was named for the hobo's utopia of the song. But the ascent does offer a good conditioner. Perhaps not as startling as "cigarette trees, bushes ready with handouts, and cops with wooden legs," the secluded lane is ideal for a hot day, tunneling through cool hemlock and firs shading wildflowers and ferns.

Drive Interstate 5 to Aberdeen exit west (US 101, State 8) out of Olympia. About 10 miles a sign appears for Rock Candy Mountain Road, along with Summit Lake. Turn left across the highway, and pick up a dirt lane going left, then right, to ascend gradually.

The road threads between cliffs draped with ferns, then through woods of huge, gray-dappled alder and droopy hemlocks and firs, the trunks covered with moss. The biggest wildflowers and skunk cabbage hide in far, moist reaches beyond tangled brush and fallen logs. Bear left at a Y fork, and in nearly 2 miles is a rustic sign, "Rock Candy Mt. Entrance," by a yellow gate (usually open). The single-lane, dirt road continues with holes and (in early spring) muddy

areas to a powerline junction 1½ miles from the gate. Take the left fork uphill. Another fork appears almost immediately. Go left again on narrower road (marked Capitol Peak) about 3 miles, where a narrow jeep track heads left uphill. Park here and begin walking. Do NOT attempt to drive farther — impossible ruts appear later and there are no turnouts where it is bad.

About 1½ miles the road splits. Keep ascending right. (The left goes downhill to a dead-end.) The climb continues gently for another mile, with a last short, steep lunge for the top. No streams, so carry water. The grassy knob on the top of the little peak is a deer-and-elk hunters' camp. Views are not as encompassing as from nearby Big Larch Mountain, but the fringe of firs screening the lookout to the northwest shelters a grassy table for a picnic lunch.

If there is time and plenty of energy for another Black Hills peak, the hiker may continue south on the Capitol Peak Road 3 miles to the Big Larch Mountain Road — see Hike 95. But the road is rough and not recommended for passenger cars.

Round trip 5 miles
Allow 3½ hours
High point 2364 feet
Elevation gain 764 feet
Best March to November, often good in winter
Jeep road

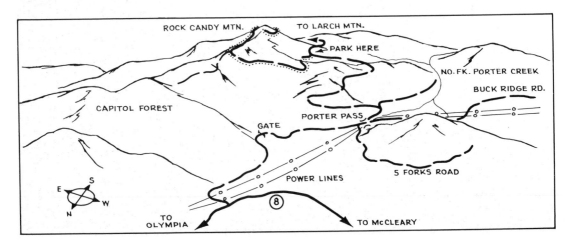

Bleeding heart on road to Rock Candy Mountain

93 MILLERSYLVANIA STATE PARK

Because an Austrian royal officer fell in love with a princess and dared all to spirit his sweetheart away to exile in America, we are left a legacy of beauty.

Many rumors circulated around John L. Miller and his wife, Anna Barbara, when they came to Washington Territory in 1881 and purchased land. But Miller was a man of mystery. A few papers, and a yellowed clipping he left when he died, indicated he had been a bodyguard of Franz Josef I of Austria, had served as a general in his army, and had brought the emperor's daughter, Anna Barbara, as his wife to this country. The surviving son of the couple's three children, F. J. X. Miller, willed 775 acres in 1924 to the state, to preserve as virgin forest. Miller logged his stands, but selectively, so many giants that he spared still stand in Millersylvania State Park. (The park's present total acreage is 833.)

Drive Interstate 5 south about 8 miles south of Tumwater and take exit off right at sign for Maytown and Millersylvania State Park. (Also marked Little Rock). Follow underpass east past Maytown 2 miles to intersection with Tilly Road. Turn left ½ mile to park entrance. Follow signs from the park entrance to the boat launch at lake. Park here, near two barred dirt tracks. Take the path behind a log barrier. The other is posted and kept exclusively for organized group camp members.

One can hike for hours and never get lost on this park's 15 miles of trails and logging roads. A rail fence is the boundary line of the park anywhere. If you hit it, turn back.

In about 100 feet a timber bridge spans Spruce Creek and the path forks. For a very short hike go right. It comes out on a fire service road and ends at the campground. For longer hikes, continue on the left branch of the jeep road past alders and big cedars. In about ½ mile, a narrower path cuts into woods on the right. Almost opposite, a trail also is seen going left. The two forays make a delightful, 1-mile hike. Walk the left trail first a few hundred feet.

The trail follows an old railway grade passing between 5-foot earth banks for logging trains which hauled Miller's trees to the lake. A huge stump and several huge, living firs on the right bank indicate his selective logging. Old-growth Douglas firs 400 years old or more blot out the modern world above sword fern, bracken, Oregon grape, Solomon's seal, and berry vines.

Then return and take the trail on the right — a deep-woods trek through a forest of old giants, some blackened from fire, many downed

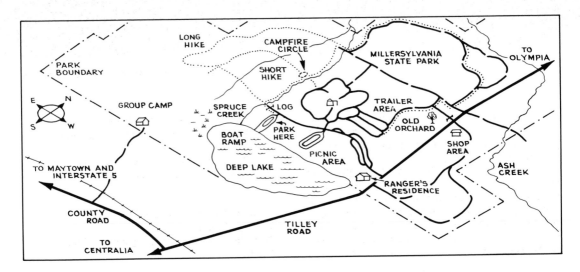

Spruce Creek, Millersylvania State Park

by storms. The trail crosses a swamp on a long, plank bridge and in almost 1 mile, reaches a trail intersection just past a campfire circle. Turn right to the car.

For a still longer hike, continue past the two trails to a triangle fork, and go right. Stay on this fire road, ignoring side roads. It crosses a creek and at nearly 2 miles comes within sight of Tilley Road. Turn right through an open, grassy area — the old Miller homestead, marked by neglected fruit trees — to the park's north end trailer area, about ¼ mile more.

The park's 240 picnic, camp and trailer sites are filled throughout summer.

Good old Miller, our royal Austrian escapist, did modern escapists a good turn.

Round trip 1 mile or 2¼ miles
Allow ½-1 hour
Best March to October, but good all winter
Dirt trail

Mount Rainier from Scatter Creek Wildlife Recreation Area

94   SCATTER CREEK RANGE

Wide as the wind and high as the stars you can almost reach. That's the prairie country south of Olympia. Ever get the urge to "cut out" and run like crazy for miles in open fields with nary an obstruction? This range, opened in 1964, is perfect — so ideal for hikers that Game Department officials wonder that it goes a-begging.

The area is available at specified times for training of hunting dogs, for organized field trials, and for grouse, duck, and pheasant hunting. See schedule below.

Drive Interstate 5 about 12 miles south of Olympia and take Maytown exit west. At Case Road turn left (south) 5 miles to Township Road. Turn right (west) to Game Department sign. Enter and park in marked area. From there, the choice is limitless. Strike off in any direction cross-field: the wide world of 750 acres awaits. Two good orientation points are a powerline that bisects the area and a large oak grove in the center.

Straight south ¼ mile from the end of the oak grove, on Township Road, is an interesting monument that marks the site of Fort Henness, built during the Indian War of 1855.

From April on, one runs through a gamut of wildflowers winking among Scotch broom and high weeds: blue lupine, buttercup, dandelions, Canterbury bells, and margarita. Wild camas, the bulbs of which the Indians used for food, are plentiful.

Take a picnic lunch and water and hike west along the service road between the parking area and the Information Officer's house to a Y fork at the corral, about .2 mile. Go right or left. If right, the track is visible, but becomes fainter with distance. Go under the powerline about ½ mile until it meets another faint track lining up with the far end of the oak grove. Cut south to the grove, about ¼ mile. Under the tall oaks are numerous delightful shady lunch nooks. Circle the grove (¾ mile) and return to the corral either by the outer road or an inside cross-field track.

Along the creek are picnic tables and many rewards: a variety of hawks and owls (particularly in winter); wood ducks, hooded mergansers, pintails, mallards, golden eye. A blue heron might appear. Once a rare snowy owl was seen. Depending on time of year and how long one sits, beavers, weasels, deer, occasional bobcat, mink, or otter may be seen — the latter playing with gusto when water is high in the creek. Bears sometimes scrounge for acorns in woods across the creek. The residence is the old Brewer homestead, built about 1858. Tales remembered by grandchildren were of bear shot from the doorstep, and how the family ran for the fort when the Indians came.

April through May, when there is no hunting, are excellent hiking months. Dog-training is allowed any time except nesting season, April to July. Field trials are fun to watch; weekends during February, March, August, and September. A few hunters appear in September, and December is another light month; wear bright clothing. But from October to December, hike somewhere else! The hunters trip over each other then.

Round trip 2¾ miles
Allow 2½ hours
Best April through August
Open field

Bright blue camas at Scatter Creek

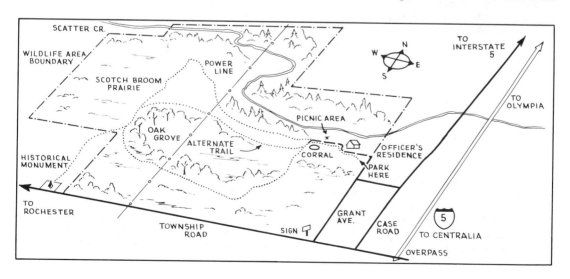

95 BIG LARCH MOUNTAIN

Though vast clearcuts are not everyone's taste in hiking terrain, Big Larch Mountain offers a fascinating walk along an old railroad grade through country logged in the old days and ways. The climax is an outdoor Cinerama of spectacular, panoramic views.

Drive Interstate 5 10 miles south from Tumwater to "Little Rock" exit. Continue west through Little Rock, over a railroad and tiny bridge, then uphill. Leave the pavement where it swings left at the top and turn right on Waddell Creek road. Continue past Margaret McKenny Park 4½ miles to Waddell Creek Junction (triangle) connecting with the main road for Delphi. Turn left for Capitol Peak.

For an alternate approach, take Aberdeen exit (US 101, State 8) west out of Olympia and within a mile exit south on Delphi-Black Lake road. In about 6 miles turn right on graveled road at Delphi entrance to Capitol Forest (sign). In 3 miles is Waddell Creek Junction. Bear right

Old railroad trestle on Larch Mountain

for Capitol Peak.

About 3 miles from the junction a sign, "Capitol Peak Truck Road," marks a wide turnout for a sharp right turn (near junction with Porter-Sherman Valley Road). Now consider two alternative routes: For a longer, more gradual climb nearly 9 miles on a new road, with more open views and interesting interpretive signs about early-day logging, continue straight through. For a shorter, steeper and rougher route on a narrow, closely-wooded road about 3½ miles, turn right on truck route. Both roads arrive at a ridge-top junction from which a steep road takes off to abandoned Capitol Peak Lookout. An interpretive sign, "Capitol Forest Vista," marks this junction.

Views are great from here west and south over the Indians' "Klahle" or Black Hills and east to Mount Rainier, with little Blumaer Hill near Tenino serving as its footstool.

Bypass the lookout road and go right downhill ½ mile. Turn left at sign for Larch Loop Road. At less than ½ mile, a stream pours down inside a sharp left curve, the last water supply. Here are remains of a burned railroad trestle, haunting reminder of fires that repeatedly swept the clearcuts, completing the job of wiping the surrounding hills clean. Continue about ½ mile; park where a narrow lane snakes uphill right. A deep rut bars further traffic.

Hike as far as you like on this old railway grade, part of more than 100 miles of railroad that crisscrossed the Black Hills when they were denuded by "highball" logging many decades ago. The long slopes falling away from the cloud-high path may still look barren, but a closer look reveals young noble firs building a new forest. The wide and easy-walking grade rounds the mountain 4½ miles almost on a level to an abrupt end, adding view on view. Vestiges of the railroad are everywhere. Rusty spikes protrude from huge stumps bearing ax-cut notches for springboards. Between infrequent loading platforms marked by huge crumbling logs, the trail is solidly flanked by colt's foot, a flower that flourishes in open and burned-over areas. Here and there a startled grouse flushes from a jackstraw of weathered gray logs; eagles and hawks glide from the peak above and soar into the valley below; on the trail are signs of larger game.

The "strip photo" views click from green, rolling hills in the west to the Olympics northwest. From a natural platform at trail's end an unbelievable 320-degree panorama spreads a relief map of lower Puget Sound's bays and inlets. Prominent to the northeast are Totten Inlet, with tiny Steamboat Island at its tip and Eld Inlet, right.

Round trip 9 miles
Allow 4½ hours
High point 1600 feet
Elevation gain 150 feet
Best March to November, often good in winter
Dirt trail

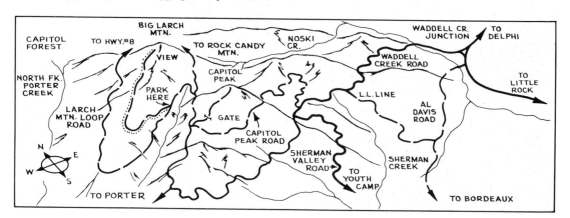

Air view of Mima Mounds

96   MIMA MOUNDS

Almost as many theories have been proposed to explain Mima Mounds as there are mounds. A phenomenon to see at least once, maybe to add your own theory.

Until early 1967, however, it seemed no theory mattered. Highways, railways, farmers' homes, fields, grazing cattle and sheep, and lately vicious little motorbikes have been rapidly ironing out the 900,000-odd hillocks dotting 30,000 acres between the towns of Little Rock, Gate, Grand Mound, Tenino, and Offut Lake. Luckily, concerned conservationists scored at least a partial victory to save them.

The mounds can be seen easily from various highways throughout the area. To get an idea of their extent, cruise a bit of the area first.

Drive Interstate 5 south to exit marked South Tumwater-Tenino. At end of off-ramp, at Trosper Road stop sign, follow Tenino sign left across freeway one block to "Old 99." Turn right (south) here for Tenino. About 8 miles, slow down. Mounds appear suddenly. Park on the shoulder for a long look over the rounded humps—heights vary from 1 to 7 feet. (Do not walk into the fields here; it is private land.

For the site of the National Registered Landmark, drive 4½ miles more to Tenino. Mounds appear and disappear, often among heavy forests. Go across Interstate 5 to Grand Mound and Rochester, then north on State 801 to Little Rock; turn left (west) on road through town, over a railroad, up a hill, through woods about 1½ miles. Just out of the forest, more fields of mounds appear. The area on the right (west) is the part marked and set aside. Park near triangle at next road intersection (to Bordeaux) and walk along the edge of the field, north or west.

Originally, The Nature Conservancy leased 548 acres of the mounds from the State Department of Natural Resources as a move to protect them from urban encroachment. Later, the National Park Service declared the Mima Prairie a Registered Natural Landmark. Last November, the lease was transferred to Evergreen State College for study purposes. To avoid interruption or detriment to botanical experiments, visitors

are asked not to walk into the field. Those with special interest, however, may call Steven Herman, Botany Department, 753-3965 at the College (Olympia, Wash.) in advance, for permission and directions on location of best specimens.

Even viewing from the perimeter, one feels the uncanny silence enveloping the mounds. Look over them, and dream up a theory.

Like Lieutenant Wilkes (1841) — Indian burials? Or an early fur company trader — volcanic origin? Or George Gibbs (1854) — spreading plant roots? Louis Agassiz (1870s) — sucker fish? LeConte (1873) — erosion? Early pioneers — buffalo mounds? Zoologists-geologists of the 1940s — a vanished race of gophers? Or the latest — a complex dirt-and-ice interaction at the foot of a dying Pleistocene glacier?

Mine? Take-off platforms for a flying saucer armada.

Round trip 10 yards to 10 miles, your choice
Allow at least ½ hour
Good anytime
Dry fields, crusty grass

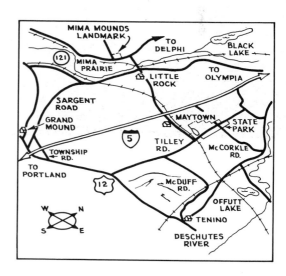

97 PENROSE POINT STATE PARK

A dwindling treasure of public beaches and woods has the natural effect of alerting a populace to appreciate those they still retain. Within recent years, Penrose State Park has been "discovered" by mariners and nature students alike. With a safe harbor, a mile or more of beach for picnics, clamming, hiking, swimming, water-skiing, and sailing, with trails and 85 campsites set among acres of Nature's arboretum, the park furnishes a setting for almost any outdoor recreation desired. Small wonder this 172-acre point of land jutting into Carr Inlet is rapidly becoming a favorite spot. Take a picnic lunch and throw in a bathing suit for all-day enjoyment.

By cross-Sound ferry to Bremerton or Southworth, pick up State 16 outside Port Orchard to Purdy. Or drive Interstate 5 south to exit for Tacoma Narrows Bridge, thence north from bridge to Purdy. At Purdy, turn west on State 302, which crosses Burley Lagoon on a long bridge and goes uphill 4 miles to a junction. A sign marks Belfair-Shelton straight ahead — your route until it branches at a second junction 2½ miles farther. Follow the road south, marked Longbranch. Park signs from there are guides to a left turn in 5 miles, leading shortly to Lakebay. Beyond Lakebay .7 mile, at the top of a hill, is another left turn for the park entrance .3 mile farther.

About ¼ mile past the park gate, the pavement splits. Turn left for the boat dock, parking area, and overnight camp area; turn right a few yards to another large parking area by the swimming beach and bathhouse. Park in either area and begin the day's hike in the woods between the two. A trail skirts the outer lip of the bluff among big madronas hanging over the waters of Mayo Cove. Another bores deeper into woods, closer to the road.

At the bathhouse, continue the beach walk to the end of the long finger of land named Penrose Point for an early resident. A few acres at the tip of this point are outside park boundary but so far park authorities have had no objections from private owners. Please do not betray this trust by bad outdoor manners. Continue around the point and head south on the other side. (Be careful of poison oak — a few clumps grow along here.) About ¼ mile, a dirt road marked "Cable Crossing" comes downhill out of the woods. Turn inland here. The road climbs an easy grade and swings westward to end at the parking lot by the bathhouse. The total so far for both woods and beach hike is 2½ miles. Another 1½ miles may be added by continuing ¼ mile farther south, past the road marked "Cable Crossing." Watch for a trail cutting into the woods. It winds across the slope of the park's south boundary and comes out near the park entrance gate. Or, about halfway, turn off right on a branch trail that cuts across to end also at the parking lot by the bathhouse.

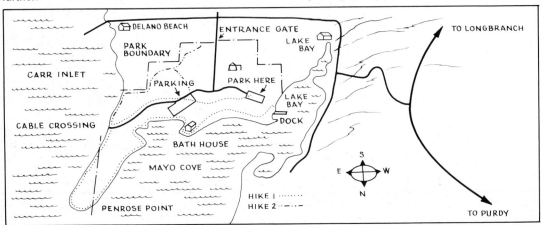

Many nature-study groups of various ages follow the trails for the wide range of Northwest plants to be found and identified. Big cedars and Douglas firs are found on the hillside, with alder, maple, and madronas along the waterfront. Huckleberry, salal, and ferns form underbrush for deer, bears, squirrels, and furry wood folk. Along the waterfront, especially near the point, are yew, maple, and madronas of imposing size and esthetic composition. Bordering the "Cable Crossing" road, banks of tall, lacy ocean spray, big leaf aralia, and berry bushes shade myriads of spring and summer wildflowers, with big puffball mushrooms popping soundlessly among them.

Penrose Park may be small, but it is packed with variety for any short-term "R&R" escapist.

Round trip 4 miles
Allow 2½ hours
Good anytime
Dirt trail, road, and beach of sand and rocks

Trilliums along a Penrose State Park trail

98   TWANOH STATE PARK

As sure as your dog's welcoming tail-wag, any newcomer to the Northwest starts his exploration of Hood Canal with Twanoh State Park. With 82 camps and 10 trailer sites, a supervised swimming beach, kitchens, picnic tables, and stoves overlooking peaceful "canal" waters (a misnomer — it is not a canal but an 80-mile-long channel from Admiralty Inlet) this state park, one of Washington's largest and most popular, annually draws thousands of campers and picnickers.

And a dollar to one Hood Canal shrimp, not more than 20 percent of all those thousands know any more about Twanoh than its "front door."

What lies at the back door? A network of 3 miles of trails over forested hill and glade, easily ranking as one of the state's most beautiful nature walks.

From Seattle, take a cross-Sound ferry to Bremerton or Southworth and pick up State 3 going south to Belfair. At the junction a mile south of Belfair, turn west on State 106. Or drive west across Tacoma Narrows Bridge, north from the bridge to Purdy, then west on State 302 to the junction mentioned.

Following Hood Canal on its south side the winding drive is garnished with attractive cottages bearing individualistic names like "Idlours." Turn shoreward off highway at park sign, about 7 miles from the junction, and leave the car in parking area.

To explore the backyard, start across the road, on the west side of the creek. To avoid confusion, think of the trail network as one long loop reaching into the woods from the highway, with an interconnecting trail about midway. The long trail skirts "round the mountain"; the midway connection cuts from hilltop to creek bottom over a steep series of switchbacks.

Follow the wide path along the creek. A veritable Eden seems to sprout with superlatives: the tallest of devil's club, the thickest of moss and ferns, the biggest of old stumps, the most enticing of gravel bars, most fragrant of cedars, and most delicate of wildflowers in the lush creek bed.

At not quite ½ mile, in an open, grassy spot, a faint trail and sign mark the junction of the interconnecting switchback trail; however, continue along the creek. The path ascends gradually, rising higher above the singsong stream and its lovely greens, then switchbacks sharply, climbing to open mountainside covered with huckleberries. About 1¼ miles from the switchback trail-end by the creek is the other end on the top of the hill, where the trail crosses the dead-end of the fire-service road. Continue a few feet; the trail crosses the fire road again before descending to the creek.

To shorten the hike, follow the fire road down to the highway. But the switchback trail is far more picturesque and romantic: soughing of wind through big firs and hemlocks, sunlight burnishing huckleberry leaves to gold, then red; when the path is damp, animal tracks for that wild touch.

After the fourth hairpin turn, on the last lap, watch for an old, rotted tree whose 4-foot-

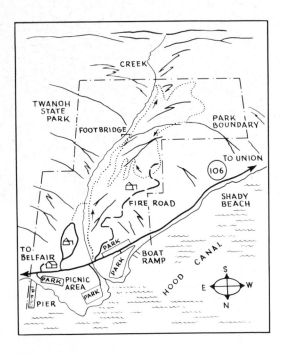

Forest trail at Twanoh State Park

thick trunk still stands, though its base is chewed down to about 8 inches.

Coming out by the creek to the highway again, one knows Twanoh has more than meets the eye at its front door.

Round trip 3 miles
Allow 2½ hours
Good all year
Dirt-and-gravel path

99 LOST CANYON OF THE SKOKOMISH

Climb to a plateau where the world seems to stand still and the silence is so exquisite it rings in your ears. Sunlighted bear grass studs a field with globes of silver-green hoarfrost, swaying like tiny lamps atop thin stems over clumps of coral-tinted Indian paintbrush. Suddenly a wide, deep canyon yawns open beside the road. A moment's pause; a look into a strange, tight valley; then one drops down, down. A delicious, rare sensation grows: You are an explorer, far in the hinterland. You have discovered a "Lost Canyon." A Tarzan howl and a few thumps of the chest are in order.

Mount Ellinor, left, and Mount Washington, center, from overlook above the Lost Canyon of the Skokomish. Note Washington's profile. The General is lying down. The highest point is his chin, next his nose, and then his sloping forehead.

Sure — civilization is just next door. No matter. This hike satisfies the conquistador urge.

Take cross-Sound ferry to Bremerton or Southworth; pick up State 3 south to Belfair and US 106 to Union, then north on US 101 along Hood Canal. At Potlatch State Park, turn left on narrow gravel service road at the south edge of the trailer-camp site, opposite shoreside picnic area. After a steep climb, the rough gravel road levels in 1½ miles and passes under a powerline, and at .6 mile meets the Stevens Road intersection. A forest road sign (SH F-1400) marks it but the direction intended is vague. Continue west, straight across the intersection (to the left is Stevens Lake). The surrounding area is part of a Christmas tree farm, and small firs bear the marks of careful trimming. At 1½ miles, by a plateau spiked with bear grass, a deep green canyon appears on the right. Jagged, snowy peaks of Mounts Washington and Ellinor loom above smoke-blue Prospect Ridge to the north. Swiftly the road snakes down off the crest and the canyon mysteriously reappears on the left. At about 2 miles from Stevens Road intersection is a wide shoulder overhang, site of a hunter's camp. The view is like one from the prow of a ship, sighting deep into ocean troughs.

From here the road is rough, narrow, and steep, so park off the curve and begin the hike. Breathe deeply of firs and pines and walk softly around curves; a big deer may be waiting to look over intruders.

Near bottom, the road winds left into a small, pleasant valley and in just under a mile reaches a fishermen's camp at the North Fork of the Skokomish River — shallow and creek-size at this point. From June on, it can easily be waded. (But the water is cold and the rocks slippery with no purchase for bare feet. Zoris at least help maintain balance.) Local fishermen describe huge beaver ponds found by wading up-creek to the right. Beyond the creek, the dirt track divides. Turn left and walk another mile on a narrow dirt logging road. It tunnels through close second-growth forest that soon blocks the view of the river and hides huge stumps cut in earlier days.

Round trip 4 miles
Allow 2½ hours
High point 600 feet
Elevation gain 440 feet
Good all year
Dirt road

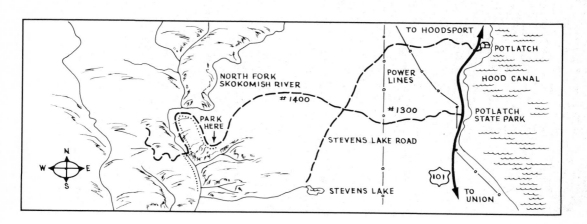

100 DOW MOUNTAIN

In the old days, the usual way of having your tag hung on a piece of landscape was to be a friend of an explorer like Captain Vancouver, who clapped friends' and officers' names on mountains, rivers, and bays as he sailed up the Sound. The only other way was to discover or settle on your own piece of land. So it was that many of our Northwest features were named, including Dow Mountain. John Dow, an engineer for the U.S. Forest Service until his death in 1910, homesteaded on a creek which headed high on a mountain west of Hood Canal. The creek and mountain now bear his name.

The mountain was logged off in his lifetime, but the face of the earth as seen from his mountain top has changed even more since then, for now Lake Cushman appears where once was the river.

Drive US 101 to Hoodsport on Hood Canal. Turn west in town on highway marked for Lake Cushman. At not quite 4 miles, turn right at a sign, "Lake Cushman Recreational Area." A smaller, separate sign marks Dow Mountain Road. Park near realty office and begin hike. Carry water; little appears above. The road soon leaves the houses behind as it narrows and snakes uphill.

The steep climb is brightened with yellow violets and starflowers in spring, and in late June and July with wild rhododendrons. The flowers provide a welcome pretext for frequent rests; the first 2 miles are a stiff climb. After the first ½ mile, the road levels briefly where views open to the south and east, improving continually, then the road heads for sky again. There are several forks, but the route, always uphill, is obvious. It hugs the east side of the hill, then, halfway to the lookout, tops the crest of a ridge, opening new views to the west, over Lake Cushman to the Olympic peaks.

Striding along the ridge top is like walking on the roof of the world. Pure yodeling country. Then another briefer climb to the top for 360-degree views. The former lookout tower is gone but a ring of white rocks, 30 feet in diameter marks a helicopter landing area on the knoll for fire fighting.

To become oriented, it's much more fun to take along a state road map, our photographer suggests. You won't need a compass. Lay the map on the ground and line up Lake Cushman with Mount Rainier. Everything else falls into place. The rocky crag east of Lake Cushman is Lightning Peak — rugged-looking with its snowy wrap in spring and early summer. West of the lake, Mount Ellinor and Mount Washington dominate the skyline.

Trace the colossal profile Mount Washington thrusts into the sky. The father of our country lies on his back, with his feet toward Mount Ellinor. The highest point is his sharp chin. Second highest point, slightly lower, is his famous

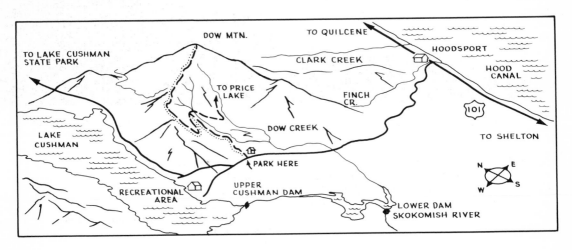

Lake Cushman and Lightning Peak from Dow Mountain

nose, followed by his sloping forehead.

For some reason, Mount Washington was left out of Olympic National Park, and so—tragically—it has no protection. The Big Creek logging road, cut almost to timberline, leaves a giant scar on its side.

Round trip 8 miles
Allow 5 hours
High point 2675 feet
Elevation gain 1927 feet
Best April to October, often earlier and later
Gravel road

INDEX

Youngs Creek

INDEX · Continued